Notes from the *Eye* of the
Storm

TO CHRIS.
THANK YOU FOR
WHAT YOU DO.

Samuel Gorrison

Notes from the *Eye* of the
Storm

A Memoir

Samuel Davisson

B.A. B.S. M.Div. M.D.

Matador
5 Weir Road
Kibworth Beauchamp
Leicester LE8 0LQ, UK
Tel: (+44) 116 279 2299
Fax: (+44) 116 279 2277
Email: books@troubador.co.uk
Web: www.troubador.co.uk/matador

ISBN 978 1848765 306

British Library Cataloguing in Publication Data.
A catalogue record for this book is available from the British Library.

Typeset in 11pt Palatino by Troubador Publishing Ltd, Leicester, UK

Matador is an imprint of Troubador Publishing Ltd

Printed in Great Britain by the MPG Books Group, Bodmin and King's Lynn

DEDICATIONS

For my wife and daughter
You make everything worthwhile.

For my father
Thank you for being absolutely incorruptible.

For the nurses
Without you the heart of medicine would be lost.

For the Paramedics
You are true professionals in absolutely impossible circumstances.

For the Volunteer Emergency Medical Technicians and Firemen
The depth of a community's soul can be measured by the strength of its volunteer services.

For Margaret
Without your dedication and technical expertise, this project would never have come to completion.

TABLE OF CONTENTS

INTRODUCTION

Fountains Abbey, North Yorkshire, England
25 June 2009

D emons! As if life wasn't tough enough, now we have demons. I know they exist because I've been looking at some thirteenth century religious manuscripts in the Fountain's Abbey Museum. In the margins of the holy writ, a monk has drawn a little cartoon demon. That demon is a very busy guy. On one page the demon is whispering impure thoughts into the ear of a monk who is standing unsteadily on a balance beam between heaven and hell. On another page, similar demons are using long metal hooks to pull a monk towards Satan's lair. The closest I ever came to that was when a six foot seven inch state cop pulled me over because my vehicle registration had expired.

It only took a short period of time for me to appreciate how real those demons were to the monks who created them 900 years ago. For those monks daily life was a struggle between the forces of heaven and hell. There may be a bit of truth in that perception, but on the whole, their lives were caught up in a whirlpool of superstition. Fear must have been their constant companion. However, even in those unenlightened times, there must have been a few brave men and women who tried to get beyond the falsehoods that were continually being spoon fed to the masses. My assumption is that those courageous souls would have attempted to ground themselves in consistent observable realities which all of us are exposed to on a daily basis. But that kind of exploration was not for the faint of heart. Without data resulting from centuries of applied scientific method, any departure from the most commonly travelled ideological road must have been terrifying. How could anyone know that their innermost thoughts and feelings were not the work of these little demons that flutter about on the same pages that contain the very word of God? Step too far out of line and you could end up lighting someone's garden at night.

In the early sixteenth century, the monks encountered a very real demon. Much to everyone's surprise, many of the abbeys had become wealthy. That was not the intent of the poor monks who originally founded those monasteries. But as time went on, many elderly and wealthy nobles were worried about the fate of their immortal souls in the afterlife. In order to deal with that concern, those same nobles donated large tracts of land to the monasteries. They were hoping that the resulting grateful prayers offered by the monks would move their souls closer to heaven. It was a pure and simple business deal with theological underpinnings. All of that new land combined with hard work and good farming techniques resulted in money pouring into the abbeys. That made the abbeys a very ripe plum for a bankrupt King Henry VIII. Henry made his move. He embarked on what British historians call the "dissolution" of the monasteries. "Dissolution" represents a very sanitized term. It sounds like Henry just added water to the monasteries and dissolved them. What he really did of course was take these magnificent hand built structures and pull them down. What he couldn't pull down he blew up. Then he plundered the abbey's gold, silver and land. Henry did offer many of the monks made homeless by the dissolution a stipend or a pension. But Henry's thirst for absolute power was unrelenting. Those religious leaders who continued to affirm the Pope as having supreme religious authority in England were executed for treason. The remaining religious leaders who chickened out rapidly made the transition to the new politically correct Church of England. It was a brutal and unstable situation at best.

Speaking of the Church of England, about a decade ago I found myself driving home late at night following a medical conference just outside of London. I turned on the car radio in order to catch the 11.00 pm BBC news. The newsreader presented the usual list of horrific world events. But the BBC saved the most interesting news story for last. Somewhere in the West Country, a small group of parishioners had uncovered a midnight liturgical church service. All of the vicars presiding over that service were wearing dresses. All the worshippers, both male and female, were wearing dresses as well. Local church officials were

2

currently forming a committee that would debate what should be the appropriate Christian response to this situation. Oh my! Where are the cast members of Monty Python when you really need them? Can you imagine John Cleese bumbling his way through that committee? He would be wearing a three piece suit and a woman's hat. He would then stand up and ask the committee "Well, were the vicars really wearing dresses or were they just pants suits?" Michael Palin would be dressed in drag as an old woman sitting in a corner. He would be knitting furiously and muttering under his breath "Guillotine, GUILLOTINE!!!"

Can't turn your back on those demons!

Chapter I

SQUARE ONE

The Jared Coffin House, Nantucket,
April 2005

B urnt. In other words, toasted to a crisp. The combination of stress resulting from my emergency room work combined with fatigue from post radiation illness has brought me to my knees. I have never known stress to be physically painful, but it is now. So, with apologies to my very supportive family, I placed a few simple things into a bag and hopped on a ferry to Nantucket.

In any sort of stressful life situation you must find a place where they can't get you. A healing atmosphere arises out of physical distance from your problems, combined with beautiful surroundings and a light dusting with fine red wine. It was also crucial to find an old porch with creaking floorboards along with a vintage rocking chair facing the sun on an otherwise cool day. You can then wrap up in a toasty blanket, lean your head back on the rocker and kiss the world goodbye. Then the layers of stress can slowly begin to peel away from your soul.

I found myself drawn to Nantucket because of its incredible history. For over 150 years, Nantucket was the center of the early American whaling industry. Nantucket's whaling boats set sail for three to five years at a time. Regardless of how you may feel about hunting whales, it took incredible courage to make those journeys. Less than a hundred feet from where I am sitting, a former first mate told a young author about his struggle for survival after an enraged bull sperm whale repeatedly rammed and sunk his ship. The young author was Herman Melville and the saga of Moby Dick was born.

In contrast, the voyage of my own life is drawing to a close. It doesn't look like I have a lot of time left. How then, does one begin again when the sun is setting? What can provide a context dynamic enough to breathe life into the end of life? I began to find the answers to those questions by walking Nantucket's off season beaches. I was out there alone. Some part of me resonated with the timeless quality present in the pounding surf. I found myself recalling past events that became my life's story. Reviewing the past somehow allowed me to start over in the present.

Initially, I found myself flooded with memories of my time at Union Theological Seminary in New York City during the early 1970s. Those were turbulent times at the Union. Something called "German Form Criticism" had made it clear that we may never be able to separate what Jesus actually said from the sayings of the early church. Apparently the early Christians expected a rapid second coming of Christ. As the first generation of Christians began to die out, someone said "Hey, maybe we should write down what occurred during Jesus' life". The earliest gospel, Mark, is a patchwork of historical sources put together decades after Christ's' crucifixion. The later gospels Mathew and Luke built on Mark and expanded the commentary. Did you ever notice that the virgin birth is missing from the gospel of Mark? Did the editor of Mark just forget about that little immaculate incident?

Besides the controversy behind biblical historical accuracy, my Seminary had another problem. There was a lot of faculty political infighting, which seems to be an inevitable part of any large religious institution. There was the old theological guard and the new theological guard. I won't even go into that.

Running concurrent with the traumas at Union was the Vietnam War. Fundamental disagreements about the war were tearing the fabric of United States society apart. Many of the students, myself included, got actively involved in the anti-war movement. I went with a large group from the United Council of Churches, placed the name of a dead Vietnamese civilian on my chest, lay down in Richard Nixon's driveway, and refused to move. We, in theory, represented the Vietnamese villagers who died needlessly during the war.

The United Council of Churches notified the D.C. Police far in advance that this would be a non-violent demonstration. To be honest, it was a bit unnerving to lie down on the Whitehouse driveway. I felt I had crossed a line. But rather than waste a golden opportunity, the police used new recruits to carry us away. They knew no one would get hurt, so they might as well give the recruits some experience. I remember laying there with my eyes shut (I was supposed to be dead) and hearing a platoon of police officers marching up to my location. "Oh Oh" I thought. But all went according to plan. I spent the night in the D.C. lockup with my New Testament professor as a cell mate. A combination of bolony sandwiches, steel beds and a cell door that closed with a definitive finality let us know we were going nowhere. I really admired my New Testament professor and thought this would be a great opportunity to discuss the real issues of our faith. He looked at me and said "I have a terrible headache." and went to sleep. In depth dialogue would have to wait.

New York City of the early 1970s was the scene of unlimited tolerance. Many of my friends were mugged. You just walked at a quick pace on the streets, did not make eye contact, and hoped the muggers picked someone else. It's no wonder the elderly fled to Florida. The lawlessness of the 1970s was horrifying.

Here's the irony. Being a Vietnam veteran saved my life in New York City. Late one evening, burdened down with text books, I made my way to my girlfriend's apartment in Brooklyn. I decided to be as safe as possible and travel a major road that had street lights. A tall, thin Hispanic man carrying a shopping bag walked briskly past me in the opposite direction. Immediately afterwards I heard rapid footsteps closing in behind me. In Vietnam you always knew who or what was around you. The enemy hid until they were ready to strike. I spun around to face him only to watch the blunt end of a hatchet head bounce off my chest. He was trying to bring the hatchet blade down between my right shoulder and neck. When I spun around, he pulled back and the hatchet fell short. He backed away and cursed at me under his breath. Still holding my books with my left hand I patted my chest looking for blood. He then put his hatchet back into his shopping bag and strode away. I quickly found a payphone. Two police detectives arrived just after my attacker disappeared into the subway. We drove around for a bit looking for him, but of course he was gone. After a while the detectives actually began to doubt my story. These guys were not Briscoe and Green from "Law and Order".

Well intentioned ideals often get altered when you realize there are people to whom your life means absolutely nothing. Conscientious objector during the Vietnam war notwithstanding, if I had been armed, I would have shot my assailant. I am absolutely convinced that having missed me, he went and killed someone else.

Speaking of the police at that time, as part of my later medical training, I got a tour of the lower East Side morgue right next to Bellevue Hospital. I watched as two detectives spoke to a medical examiner who was probing an obvious knife wound that penetrated the abdomen of a tall, handsome and dead middle aged, black male. My guess is that the blade probably lacerated his liver causing fatal internal bleeding. The fact that the blade came up into his liver meant that the assailant was most likely a woman. Women tend to stab in an upward motion; men, with more chest strength, tend to stab downward. I heard one detective say "You know doc, if you call this a homicide, we'll have to do an investigation".

In the same large room was a dead baby laying next to a short Hispanic chap with a bullet wound in his throat which resulted in the back of his head being blown off. Added to these cases was a huge room filled with a whole host of other horrors. Into the middle of this unbelievable scene, attendants wheeled in a dead, young white woman. One of my fellow classmates, Nick, recognized her as his neighbor. She had just died of a drug and alcohol overdose. Nick did not know what to do. He was blown right out of the water.

Then as a special treat, we got a guided tour through the New York City morgue museum. You have to be an insider to get this tour. Tourists in Hawaiian shirts with sunglasses and cameras are not allowed to wander through. If it's a particularly heinous or bizarre case, it's in there. I won't go into gruesome detail. Suffice it to say, Nick and I both left with memories we didn't need.

Prior to coming to Union Theological, I had never spent much time in any big city. For reasons just stated, the rancid beef stew that was New York City in the early 1970s was a rude awakening. But within that dangerous context, Union did provide us with a few great learning experiences. To Union's credit, they placed a lot of emphasis on society's social issues. If you had any interest in working with the poor or disabled, Union would find somewhere in the city that would challenge both your beliefs and emotional endurance.

I knew part way into the first year that I could no longer follow a pathway that was limited to sterile classrooms, so I volunteered to work in one of New York City's single room occupancy hotels. This needs a bit of explaining. By the 1970s, New York City had taken over a number of large old mid town hotels. Each hotel room was about 12 feet by 8 feet. There was a bed, a counter for a hotplate, along with a small refrigerator, a table and little else. The people in these hotels had all hit hard times. For many it was the end of the road. Most of the occupants of the hotels had been assigned to a social worker who helped them sort out the basics of everyday living. The students from Union came in and did whatever we could to help out. For some of us it was the beginning of a lifelong ministry to the poor.

I was providing some guitar music for the weekly Sunday religious service that was held in the hotel's basement. During the service, one of the social workers asked if any of us had a medical background. I was only a few months away from my army medical experience, so I asked what was going on. Apparently an elderly woman had passed out in her room upstairs and they wanted someone to stay with her until the ambulance arrived. I offered to help.

Entering a small, somewhat dingy room, I found a likewise somewhat disheveled lady in her 70s. She had a heavily wrinkled thin face, unkempt straight salt and pepper hair that just touched her shoulders, cigarette staining on her fingertips and a nightgown that was not bought yesterday. She was lying quietly in her bed, too weak to sit up. I introduced myself. She knew I was from the seminary. She said "I can't talk to you, you're too good". I replied "I'm not as good as you think I am". She retorted "Say a dirty word". I said "Damn". We became instant friends. Her name was Wilma.

As it turns out, Wilma had been too depressed over the previous few days to cook her own food. Her only immediate medical problem was a lack of nourishment; so I opened a can of soup and prepared it for her. Soon after eating, her strength returned.

Wilma's only contact with the outside world was a nice young gay fellow named Richard who lived down the hall. Wilma was too infirm to walk further than the bathroom, so Richard got her the required groceries and cigarettes. How Richard ended up in that hotel was never clear to me. He seemed to be functioning without any serious handicap. In return

9

for the groceries, Wilma would offer Richard advice on everyday living, which he seemed to need. Most of the other folks on the floor were borderline psychotics who couldn't quite make it outside of a protected environment.

I visited Wilma twice a week for months. As she learned to trust me, the details of her life emerged. She left school in the eighth grade and entered the school of hard knocks. But Wilma was nobody's fool and she had soon clawed her way up Hollywood's corporate ladder. Her career peaked when she became a Public Relations Director for MGM in the 1940s. Among other things, her job was to keep everyone happy by throwing lavish parties. She told me she was once propositioned by Clark Gable, but she turned him down. She said "I have regretted that decision my entire life".

At the beginning of one of her cocktail parties, Wilma panicked when she realized that she had forgotten to make arrangements for live music. She then heard some noise outside in the street. It was the local college marching band practicing for the homecoming parade the next day. She ran out into the street and threw herself in front of the band. They stopped. She offered them all they could eat and drink if they would come in and play a few marches for the party. They were a big hit. I suspect, however, that some of the students did not make it to homecoming.

Wilma's first husband died at a relatively young age which caused her to enter a period of depression. She married again, this time to a man with a drinking problem. Together they sailed down that booze laced slippery slope that only an alcoholic can adequately describe. By the time she sobered up, she had lost everything. Now elderly and in poor health, she found herself in the dingy room where we met.

She made friends with some of the other seminarians. There was more than enough of her personality to go around. Now she had a captive audience. We were supposed to be helping her, but she was much wiser in the ways of the world than any of us. Since she couldn't leave her room, she began to live vicariously through us. She had to have regular reports on our dating lives. After several reports about one girl I was dating, Wilma said "I don't like this girl; she's not for you". I responded, "But Wilma, she is so beautiful". Wilma stopped what she was doing, looked me straight in the eye and said "That fades!" This was lesson number one. Numerous lessons followed, but like a fool, I didn't write them down. Many of her wise insights have escaped my memory.

Reading was Wilma's great love. She was truly self-educated. But her visual acuity had deteriorated to the point where the written word was no longer accessible. However, Wilma's social worker rose to the occasion. Within a few weeks, Wilma's coke bottle glasses arrived. Jim, another seminarian, bought Wilma a New Testament printed in large type. As a result of Jim's efforts, Wilma (who was Jewish) read the New Testament for the first time. When she was done, I asked her what she had thought of the gospels. She replied "Do you realize that things I thought my whole life were said by William Shakespeare were really said by Jesus Christ?"

After about four months I got word that Wilma had been taken into the hospital. I arranged for flowers to be sent and was getting dressed to visit her when her social worker called. Wilma had died. I had no idea she was that ill. I was sitting on my bed crying, when for a few moments I felt her presence. I am not making this up. I have never experienced anything like that before or since. The simple message, without words, was that everything was O.K. I took great comfort from those moments.

Every young person should have a Wilma in their life; someone who is both a mentor and a friend, someone who will not come at you with cheap clichés or platitudes, but share life's lessons that always come at a price. I miss her. She is a treasured memory.

A few weeks after starting my academic work at Union, the euphoria at being back from Vietnam in one piece began to wear off. Sitting in my single dorm room, I faced a stack of books twenty inches high. I was expected to read those books.

My room was cozy. The walls were solid, about eighteen inches thick. My window faced a small dark and empty inside courtyard next to Riverside Church. The steeple at Riverside Church is almost thirty stories high and dominates the Upper West Side skyline. Father Daniel Berrigan of anti war fame said Riverside Church was where they buried God standing up.

Encased in concrete, my room was an ideal setting for some serious studying. There was no outside noise. I decided to throw myself into the books and make a determined effort to get a theological education. Within two weeks of hard reading I experienced the same draining depression I had experienced my senior year in college. My entire time in the U.S army, including Vietnam, I had been depression free. I had been scared, exhausted and frustrated in the army, but never depressed. I loved my work as an Army Medical Corpsman. For the first time in my life I had real responsibility. But now that I was at Union, it was back to academic square one. Now what!?! I had entered a three year academic program just in time to find out that I had a major block against studying. Wonderful! I realized that I needed help. I wasn't nuts, so a psychiatrist with his prescription pad didn't make any sense. Therefore I opted for psychotherapy. Going through a school referral, I interviewed with a very intelligent female psychotherapist. But her practice was full, so she referred me to a fellow graduate of the C.G.Jung Institute. He was a really nice guy. He was too nice. He smiled when he didn't mean it. He had lots of ideals. He was just like me, and that wasn't going to work. Not enough fresh air in that relationship. So I asked for another referral. I ended up in the office of another C.G.Jung graduate. He was off a kibbutz in Israel. His doctoral degree before turning to psychotherapy was in the physical sciences. He was a pure pragmatist. We could not have been more different. He was perfect.

I'll never forget his introduction to our first session. He said "Are you sure you want to do this? Once you enter the subconscious you begin an irreversible journey. Everything will change. A lot of people really don't like what they find inside themselves".

We began what for me was a pivotal five year relationship. As time went by, everything did change, albeit slowly. It can be devastating to change the underpinning of your own personality too quickly. Success in psychotherapy simply requires that you want the truth more than you want anything else. Sometimes that's a bitter pill, but the truth is the only way forward. As I said earlier, I had returned to square one. However, this square one was where I needed to be.

Even though I finished the Master of Divinity Degree and used it as a stepping stone to further my medical training, I knew by the end of the first year at Union that a career in the ministry was not for me. A Minister represents the ideals of Christianity placed within a community. But I always felt short circuited when what I was feeling had nothing to do with those religious ideals. I needed room to grow. I needed spontaneity, affirmation, confidence and the gut feeling that I had not sold out. "Selling out" means saying what you think people want to hear, or what you think you should be saying, rather than expressing what you really feel. "Selling out" in my experience happens frequently. When it does happen, life's forward progress comes to a temporary screeching halt.

Realizing that the pulpit was calling anyone other than me, I entered clinical pastoral education during my second year at Union. This turned out to be one of the most valuable academic courses of my entire life. Six of us went to a Brooklyn hospital and trained as hospital chaplains. The faculty spent a year teaching us how to listen to people. When I finally became a physician, that skill became invaluable.

Our student chaplain group was composed of a wide range of personalities and backgrounds. There was Jim who was Greek Orthodox. Jim had a problem. When you became ordained as a Greek Orthodox priest in the 1970s (I don't know what the rules are currently) you could be either single or married. However, whatever your marital status, that status could not change after you became ordained. If you were single you stayed single; married, you stayed married. Jim's ordination was coming up at the end of the year and he didn't have a girlfriend. A looming lifetime of celibacy sent him into an appropriate panic. Jim was tall, handsome, intelligent and well mannered. I could not figure out why he could not find an appropriate bride, immediately. The real problem was the urgency of his situation. Have you ever noticed that if you are content within a relationship, tempting outside offers abound? But if you radiate any sort of urgent need, members of the opposite sex avoid you like the plague. Jim's theological clock was ticking.

Tony was an Italian protestant. He was low key and sincere. Bob was a pseudo hippy about a decade too late. He was, however, a very good listener which was a crucial skill for our work. Kim was very interesting. He was a former lieutenant in the Republic of Korea (R.O.K) marines. In the 1970s the R.O.K marines were one of the most feared fighting forces in the world. Kim used to discipline his troops with a baseball bat. If, after being bludgeoned to the earth, the recruit in question jumped up and said "Please sir, can I have some more?" Kim backed off. But if the recruit stayed on the ground and whimpered, there was no mercy. Kim must have had an epiphany at some point because he was as gentle as a kitten when I knew him. But I never pushed him. Once embedded in the human personality, I don't think the baseball bat ever entirely leaves. It must be nice to know that your hospital chaplain can kill you five different ways.

Dave was from Eastern Europe. I wasn't sure why he was there. He was just a party animal and he loved women. The student nurses used to say to him "You don't act like a chaplain." But he was easy to be around.

Our Program Director was an aloof character. He kept his own emotional cards very close to his chest. I was never sure what he was feeling or thinking. Aloof or not, he was a very competent professional. We learned a great deal from him.

While working in the hospital, we got to wear the black pastor's shirt with the white clerical collar. However our white clerical collar was different from the standard issue. Our collars had a vertical black line down the center, indicating we were students. This fascinated me. I wasn't sure whether the black line represented the stain of sin that was still on my soul, or if it indicated that my tank was half empty.

During our year of clinical pastoral education, the "verbatim" was our primary learning tool. A verbatim is a literal word for word recounting of our conversations with the patients. Each of us carried a beeper. When a call came into the Chaplain's office that a patient had requested a visit, one of us would be dispatched to the bedside. Our conversations with the patient would typically last five to twenty minutes and often ended with prayer at the patient's request. We would then sit down in some quiet place with a warm cup of coffee and write down our conversation with the patient word for word as best we could remember. After a few weeks of practice, it was remarkable how accurately we could recreate that conversation. We then sat down individually with our program director and reviewed the content of our verbatim. What we learned about the patient was interesting. What we learned about ourselves from those conversations left us dumbfounded. Our own words exposed us. It was time for another cup of coffee and some genuine reflection on what had motivated us to say certain things to the patients.

As a result of listening to the patients and reviewing verbatim over a period of months, two basic points emerged that I think would apply to any counseling situation.

No.1. You can never assume how anyone will feel about anything. For example, you might wander into a hospital room where an elderly lady has just expired. Multiple family members are at the bedside. As a Chaplain it would be tempting to produce a volley of comforting platitudes. But what you don't know is that the family members are immensely relieved that the old bat finally died. You have to feel your way through these situations.

One of our guys answered a nurse's call to a bedside of a woman whose premature twins had just been stillborn. The nurses brought the babies bodies to the mother so that she could see them. Our fellow decided that it would be comforting to the mother to have the twins baptized, which he did. The mother, speaking softly in here weakened state, said something in a foreign language that he could not understand. She seemed to object. As it turned out the family was Muslim. Oops! Much heat.

No.2. If a patient starts to talk about a personal problem that the counselor has not dealt with in his own life, the counselor will immediately change the subject. That's why every councilor should undergo years of their own psychotherapy. If you haven't dealt with your own demons you won't be a very effective guide to others. Instead of helping them, you'll keep tuning out what they are trying to say.

Early on in our training I was called by the nurses to see Olga. Olga was a woman in her late sixties with severe vascular insufficiency to her legs. A few months prior to my visit, her right leg had to be surgically amputated. Now her left leg was turning black and she repeatedly refused to have the left leg amputated as well. Please understand that gangrene of the leg is not a fun way to die. It really hurts.

Olga's husband and relatives were part of a local charismatic revival church. Prayers were said, songs were sung and tambourines shaken every day at the bedside. Despite the obvious outcome with the right leg, the church members expected a miracle. The left leg would be healed. Olga just sat there stoically through the whole production. Every day the prayers got longer, the songs and tambourine got louder, and the left leg got blacker and blacker. The whole proceeding actually became a disturbance on the ward.

It took me a week to crack why Olga would not have the second leg amputated. When we were alone she stared me in the eye and said "With one leg I can still stand, while leaning against something and cook and clean. If both legs are gone I will never be able to stand. I will be placed on a chair in a corner. I will become "Olga the piece of meat"." I immediately said "Oh Olga your family wouldn't do that!" In other words, I completely cut her off. Her lack of self worth and potential abandonment by her family were too much for me to swallow. Maybe those Bible belting relatives actually would put her in storage. Who's to say? But my job at that point was to listen to her fear, and I couldn't do it.

Another question commonly presented to me by elderly patients was "What have I done that God would punish me with this horrible illness?" The easy answer would be "God doesn't work like that". The harder answer would be "Did anything happen in your life that would make you feel that God should punish you?" Then, as stated above, the trick is to be vulnerable to their answers.

Having a trained compassionate counselor in the setting of critical illness is absolutely essential. There's just no way around that. Once a patient is diagnosed as terminal, there is a tendency for the doctors to move on to patients "that they can help". It's important to realize that physicians have little or no training in dealing with patient's emotional needs. Given that physicians are often present at a person's most vulnerable moments, the absence of that training represents a huge error on the part of medical schools.

Physicians tend to be highly competitive and anal personalities who often do not ooze compassion. I always felt that the best future physicians in our medical school were not always the students with the highest grades. Instead a small contingent of our students could best be described as "junk yard dogs." They backed into medical school and were lucky to be there. Their lives were a string of outrageous stories best kept out of print. But they had tasted life. The human experience that patients present in a medical office would not be foreign to them. They had "been there and done that" and maybe learned a few things along the way. There is simply no substitute for life experience.

In addition to medical professionals potentially backing away from terminal patients, friends and relatives tend to be equally uncomfortable with what the patient has to say. After all, the patient reminds everyone of their own mortality and that's never fun. Close family members tend to burst into tears when the patient talks about their own impending death. The situation becomes so painful that the conversation dilutes itself to talking about the weather. The issues that family members really need to discuss prior to death don't get explored. Real goodbyes don't happen. Resolution of decades old conflicts don't occur and the patient is deprived of any sense of peace or resolution. Granted some dying people turn their face to the wall and don't want to talk to anyone. That's their choice. I have seen patient denials so intense that the loved ones don't even know that the illness is serious until the patient dies. That leaves nothing but a mess of unresolved issues. Besides the emotional concerns, patients' estates have not been adequately administered. Often there is no will and families don't know what to do. If you want to see the worst brought out of families, watch them fight over money. The resulting resentments last a lifetime.

Dying is an emotional process, and that process often needs professional help. A patient can unburden himself to an objective counselor in a way that he never could to his own family. That's because there is no negative fallout resulting from what the patient says.

There is another aspect to dying; it's a very lonely process. Doctors think that because they can't cure the patient they have nothing to offer. But if you can stay emotionally vulnerable to a dying patient (and that's not easy) you are providing a tremendous service. You can walk with them to the end of their journey, and the comfort provided will never be forgotten by the family.

The hospital in which I did my medical residency employed a very gifted psychotherapist and made him available to patients in the intensive care units. There were a lot of referrals for his services, mostly made by the nurses who were constantly at the patient's bedside. Many families (if not all) are dysfunctional. There is nothing like a serious or terminal illness to bring that dysfunctional behavior to center stage. At that point the professional counselor's services are invaluable.

Hospital administrators are always trying to trim budgets. Sometimes it's hard for them to see that a professional counselor is a must in a hospital. From the administrator's point of view it's just one more salary, medical and retirement benefits, etc. etc. But by allowing the patients to ventilate, a good counselor might save the hospital a law suit a year. That alone would cover a counselor's salary. Most hospitals have a psychiatric department, but they mostly see patients who need psychiatric medications. Hospitals also have Rabbis, Pastors and Muslim clerics on call, which is good. But these folks are experts in their religion. They are not necessarily trained in psychotherapeutic techniques. As things currently stand, the burden of the patient's mental health needs falls primarily on the patient's nurse.

While I was in the middle of clinical pastoral education I was dating a very upbeat girl who was a student at an all female college located on the Hudson River. The students at that school were not overly troubled with lofty ideals. They just wanted to graduate, get a job, get married and have kids, preferably in that order. But they knew how to do one thing really well. They knew how to party. I took lessons. The party began Friday night and survivors staggered home Sunday afternoon. I remember waking up one Sunday morning to an odd scraping noise. I found my way downstairs out of curiosity. The girls were shoveling beer off the floor and out the window. Now *that* was a party.

The bottom line was simple. The only way I could deal with death being thrown in my face several times a week at the hospital was to have life thrown in my face at the weekends. Without that balance I would have been overwhelmed.

In and of itself, stress is a topic about which volumes have been written. It affects all of us. One of the major markers of a successful life is a person's ability to defuse stress, or in some very creative cases make their life's stressors work for them. For example, many career E.R doctors and nurses are adrenalin junkies. They need the rush. They drink coffee to slow down. Eventually the tread wears off the tire and it catches up to them. But for years they ride the crest of an emotional wave.

The effects of stress are invariably cumulative. A string of catastrophes over time can build up potentially damaging stress levels and the piper must be paid. Stress can make you age and even die prematurely. It can also turn you into a green eyed screaming banshee that your children will learn to loath.

Post traumatic stress is also very real. During clinical pastoral education, I watched C.P.R. being done on an elderly man who had just been admitted through the emergency department. The medical resident doing the chest compressions was berating the patient's son for not having brought him to the hospital sooner. In other words "If you had brought your father to me sooner, I wouldn't have lost him." How sensitive. Nothing like laying a lifelong guilt trip on the son. Obviously the medical resident was stressed.

In my role as an observer, I had no responsibility for the patient's medical outcome. As I was watching the chest compressions being applied, I was filled with an unexpected sense of panic. Years before in Vietnam I started C.P.R on a Vietcong soldier who had hit one of our Claymore mines. Of course he died. Afterwards I went back to my base camp and had breakfast, fascinated by the fact that I felt almost nothing. Three years later, while watching the resident perform C.P.R., all the feelings that I should have had in Vietnam came to the surface. In a crisis we bury our feelings so that we can remain functional. But those feelings never really go away. They just wait for a "safe" moment when we are ready to receive them. I grabbed a cup of coffee, sat down with Bob and unloaded. I spent six months in the Vietnam jungle in a combat situation and never really felt all that bad. As I said before, the piper must be paid.

Stress takes on some interesting forms in children. "Acting out" behavior is common. But things often go a lot deeper than that. I've had several patients who cannot remember years of their childhood. It doesn't take rocket science to figure out what went on in those years.

I noticed an interesting characteristic in young women who were victims of childhood sexual abuse. Some of them had an inappropriately immature personality characteristic. They would giggle or respond as a child would respond even though they were adults. It's almost as if part of their personality development arrested at the time of the abuse.

As a physician's assistant I worked in an orphanage. We had some kids whose home situations were so bad that the kids actually stopped physically growing. One boy was raised literally in a closet. Once protective services got him out of the gulag, he came to us. Our young staff took the time to be good to him. He shot up like a weed, after having shown no growth for over two years. Stress and abuse have ways of arresting our development on many different levels. It strikes close to home. For many kids it is home.

Shortly after I was born, my mother went through a severe post partum depression with a touch of psychosis. Not an optimal environment for a newborn. Dad told me later that the doctors wanted to institutionalize her. In the 1940s however, institutionalization meant just locking someone up with the prospect of electroconvulsive therapy. Medical treatment for post partum depression was in its infancy. So, Dad kept her at home, with me. In regression forms of psychotherapy I had vague images of recoiling from a hot light. I think she hurt me. As an adult, while talking to a random individual, I would suddenly become filled with an ill defined but overwhelming fear and have to get away. This was not paranoia. Even at the time I knew that the person I was talking to did not want to hurt me. But any close physical presence had the potential to fill me with a sense of imminent danger.

One friend of mine was a victim of physical child abuse at the hands of her father. He would throw her down a flight of stairs, etc. He never touched the other siblings. It is interesting how an abuser will target one member of a family.

Even though this woman's father is now old and frail, that sense of danger never left her. I can understand the survival advantage of a child remembering the face of danger. But this ongoing and unrelenting panic reaction can be disabling.

As I got older Mom became very devoted to me. Food was always prepared, the clothes were always clean and I always got my medications for coughs and colds. She really tried. She crumbled again psychologically when I was about three years old. Dad sent the two of us back to her old family home in Ohio. That was the one place where she felt comfortable. But I didn't see her for a year. My older maiden aunt took care of me. She loved to plug into my imagination and create stories. She was very good to me.

Mom rallied again and the nuclear family moved to Cleveland, close to Dad's work. Mom and I never fought. She did have a very dry sense of humor. But I have no memory of her ever touching me. So I grew up with a desperate need for tender physical intimacy, but at the same time any closeness was potentially threatening. You can imagine the problems that created.

I spent years working through the above dilemma. Without loving and patient people I don't know what I would have done. How do you reclaim what you never had to begin with? How do you learn to trust? Healing involves a daily process of self acceptance. There is no other way to collect the solid experiences we need to not only go on, but to actually improve life.

In summary, stress is out there in its many different and damaging shapes and forms. It's amazing that we survive at all. We're all scarred. We all behave in insane ways. In fact, being sane is not being not crazy. Being sane is knowing how you're crazy and compensating for it. For example, you can look at how you screwed up your last three relationships. At the start of the fourth relationship you know what aspects of your behavior did not work the last three times. With that insight, you can try a new and maybe more productive way to relate.

We do change, but we have to be highly motivated to do so. Our humanity is the key to the whole healing process. If you're not psychotic or antisocial, trust your spontaneous thoughts and feelings. Build on them, and above all, in the words of a wonderful colleague of mine who suffered terrible physical pain from a chronic illness, "You have to find ways to be good to yourself."

Meanwhile, back at the hospital, our year of clinical pastoral education was drawing to a close. Our student group was sitting in a hospital conference room sharing experiences from our time together. But I felt like we were still using clichés to communicate, so I left the room, picked up paper and pen and found myself a private spot. I wrote an imaginary verbatim. In that verbatim I was a young patient who had just been diagnosed with gastric carcinoma. I had about three months to live. I chose Bob as the pastor I would talk to. I tried to write an honest account of that imaginary conversation. After the verbatim was completed, I just sat quietly for a while. What came out of the verbatim was my anger. I was in my sixth year of graduate and undergraduate work. I had spent my whole life preparing for life, and now I had three months to live. What a waste.

You never forget the telephone call when they tell you that your biopsies are positive. Thirty years after I wrote the above verbatim I was on the phone with my medical consultant. He was quoting all sorts of statistics and studies. My mind wandered. But in the last line of this conversation he said "Sam, if you don't do something about this, it will definitely kill you". Now he had my full attention. Afterwards I handed the phone to my wife.

Early on I had made my own cancer diagnosis. The appropriate surgery was done, things looked good and I was pronounced cured. But eighteen months later the cancer recurred. The odds of that were three out of a hundred. Why can't I hit those kind of odds on a scratch card? Now I am in real trouble.

I referred myself to an excellent radiation oncologist and spent a summer in radiation therapy. Talk about a head trip! I called the oncologist's office to make my first appointment. I said "Hello this is Dr Samuel Davisson. I wish to make an appointment to see Dr Gray." The secretary said "Certainly doctor, what's the patient's name?" There was a moment of stunned silence. Then I said "I'm the patient."

When I first walked into the Oncology waiting area, I scanned the room. Some people were either family members of patients, or patients in the early stages of their illness. They looked fine, but they weren't smiling. Other patients looked terrible. I thought to myself "What in the world am I doing here?"

On my 10th birthday, I remember looking across the southern New Jersey sand dunes to the constant and unending ocean waves. I thought to myself "I wonder if I need to worry about getting old". But I figured that the average male life span (at that time) was seventy two years. That meant I had sixty two years left. Well, my first ten years had just taken *forever*, so I didn't think I had much to worry about. A blink of an eye later and I am staring at a potentially lethal diagnosis. Now it's time to worry. Reality was settling in.

There comes a time in everyone's life when all that is precious is taken away. It can be gradual, as with old age, or sudden as with cardiac arrest, but the surrender of all that matters to us is inevitable. It is worth taking the time to look that reality squarely in the face. You don't have to be morbid. You don't have to think about death every day. But if you are able to absorb that frightening finality at least once, then it won't be such a surprise when it actually does happen to you.

There is an interesting twist to one's thinking with a diagnosis of cancer. Long term plans are scuttled. A cancer patient will say "This was a good day" and settle for that. There is also an emotional irony with a cancer diagnosis. You live with your existence suspended. It's like being on an airplane on hold over an airport. You can't land. Emotionally everything is up in the air.

When I first received my diagnosis I prayed. "Oh God save me! I have a young child!" But over two hundred thousand innocents had just perished in the Christmas tsunami. My prayers seemed somehow unfair. After all, what made me so special? So, I changed the prayer. I said "I trust you. Stand with me through this." Out of that I did receive a sense of presence and comfort. For that I am very grateful.

Toward the end of my career as a physician I found handing out a diagnosis of advanced cancer very difficult. Even though I knew it wasn't my fault that the patient was ill, I felt like an executioner. I was their doorway into an unthinkable journey of fear and suffering. I always tried to offer some hope, rather than leave them in total blackness.

You can wax eloquently about Elizabeth Kulber Ross's five emotional stages through terminal illness. But never ever try to replace the patient's fear with those five stages or any religious belief. Let the patient tell you what they feel and what they need. It's hard and terrifying work to be vulnerable to these people. But as devastating as I found these situations, I tried not to distance myself from the patient. I didn't want them to feel abandoned.

However, I eventually blew like a fuse. The stress of my own cancer left me with shell shock. In addition, the malpractice situation in my home state put physicians in great jeopardy. No one could afford adequate malpractice insurance. Every day I went to work I knew I could lose everything I own, everything I had worked for. All the above factors proved to be too much. In 2006 I walked away from medicine.

Getting back to my time in Union, the three years came and went quickly. There were a few good courses and many good people. The students were determined to go out and have a positive impact on society. After graduation many of them did just that. Their experiences molded their vision.

As previously mentioned, we studied briefly with Father Daniel Berrigan, a priest who was jailed for burning draft files. He was a poet at heart, and taught me a lot about using words to create visual images. He also was an example of unswerving commitment against forces that devalue human life.

We did a lot of work with language. For instance, you could tell that major violence was on the horizon by watching everyday language change in an effort to dehumanize the target of that violence. We were raised with the teaching "Thou shall not kill" but in any military action, we kill. Therefore, the language has to be manipulated to dull the reality of that killing. Thus North Vietnamese soldiers became "gooks" or "Charlie". German soldiers became "Huns". When you group people like that, individual human identity gets obscured. Pulling the trigger then becomes a lot easier. Let's be honest; if you knew the opposing soldier personally, knew his parents, wife and kids, you probably wouldn't shoot him.

The summers between academic years at Union provided a lot of color and excitement in contrast to the book work. A friend of mine invited me along to California to work in a migrant farm workers family clinic organized by Cesar Chavez. I had lots of reasons not to go. As I was debating whether or not to stay in New York for the summer, I noticed that I kept humming a familiar tune. I couldn't get it out of my mind. Finally I stopped to see if I could recall the lyrics. The songs refrain was "California Here I Come". I found someone to help me with the driving. We crossed the George Washington bridge and just kept going.

The farm workers family clinic was nestled in a small town in central California. The San Joaquin Valley is an amazing place. It's basically a desert that has been reclaimed by a vast and complicated irrigation system. Any fruit or vegetable will grow there. But above all, the San Joaquin Valley is hot. In July I recall walking from the clinic about a third of a mile to the local pharmacy to pick up a soda. By the time I returned to the clinic I was ready for another soda. By the end of the working day, a large frosted mug of A&W Root Beer, from the tap, over crushed ice, was worth ten times the asking price.

Our little clinic was staffed by a fine group of folk. Priests and Nuns helped out as administrators and nurses. Farm worker wives would act as nurses' assistants and translators, doing whatever was necessary to keep things going. They were warm and well mannered people. Volunteers like me came and went and filled in the cracks. Our full time physician was named John. He was truly a man for all seasons. He had tremendous emotional and physical reserves which enabled him to rise to meet any difficulty. He also refused to allow the farm workers to be demeaned in any form by anyone. His wife Dorothy was an unending source of support to all of us.

Of interest were the farm worker children. In the clinic they didn't

24

whinge or whine. There was none of this pathetic bargaining that you see in the malls between soccer moms and their pre-schoolers. "We're going to eat before we go to the toy store, O.K?" The "O.K?" is actually asking the child's permission to do whatever the parent wants done. Incredible. The farm worker kids came from a hard life. They did what their daddies told them to do. You did not hear an "O.K?"

The clinic staff had one wonderful characteristic. What was missing from all of the staff members was ambition. No one was crawling over anyone to get anywhere. Providing medical care to migrant families was simply a good and decent thing to do, and our staff applied themselves to that task. The pay was $15 per week plus food, a roof over our heads and a tank of gas. What more do you need, at least in the short term? We had a great summer.

Everybody did what they could to keep spirits high. These were tense and difficult times. The farm workers union was staging a huge long term strike. Much of the seasonal fruit and vegetable picking ground to a halt. Joining a strike was a hard choice for the migrant workers. Many of them had starving families back in Mexico. No fruit picking, no pay. The Union could only offer the farm workers minimal striker's wages.

The growers owned huge farms and were a powerful political force in the area. Seeing their fruit and vegetables rot in the fields did not go over very well. All manner of force was brought in to break the strike, including strong arm guys whose job it was to provoke fights with the farm workers. Cesar Chavez was absolutely committed to non violence. It was obviously the only way forward. When violence did erupt, Cesar would call for a three day liquids only fast in an effort to rededicate us to non violence.

One day a group of us left the clinic to join the picket lines. We were supposed to add our support to the strike, but we were also there to give medical aid in case violence did break out. I noticed there were five growers standing to one side taking in the scene. They had never seen migrant workers act as a unified force. They were not pleased. One of them said to me "You don't look Mexican". I came over to talk to them. My eyes were drawn to one of the growers who was of Japanese descent. He was in his early sixties and his English was excellent, so he had been in the U.S for a long time. I remember thinking "He's just the right age to have been interned in one of the Japanese prisoner camps that flourished in California during World War II. He should know what it's like to be a target of racism". That Japanese grower pulled me aside and said "Those Mexicans, they eat all that hot food, that's why they are so emotional".

Following that logic one can only conclude that jalapeños engender dysphoria. After digesting that piece of information, I never ate salsa prior to oral exams or meeting the girlfriend's parents for the first time. Otherwise, God knows what I might have done. I remember looking at the Japanese grower and thinking "You've obviously learned a great deal over the years."

Outside of these confrontational situations there were lighter moments. Evenings were often shared meals of beans and rice. Once in a while a few of us were able to get a weekend off. We stuffed the essentials into backpacks and headed for the High Sierras. Even though we were located just west of the Sierra foothills, it took hours of travelling on twisting roads to reach base camp. Everyone raves about Yosemite National Park, and rightly so. But if you are in the area don't miss Kings Canyon National Park. You have to drive through the great Sequoia groves to get there. The canyon itself is thousands of feet deep and spawns the Kings River, which is one of the primary sources of the previously mentioned San Joaquin Valley irrigation system.

The primary camp ground, Cedar Grove, sits on the floor of a deep valley. The elevation of that valley floor is roughly five thousand feet. That's about as high as it gets in New England. But five thousand feet represents the foothills in the Sierras. The trails that begin at Cedar Grove will carry you into another eco system at fourteen thousand feet. People sunbathe during the day and there is ice on the tent at night. It's truly wild. The park rangers now limit the number of people who enter that park each day. By avoiding excessive crowding, everyone gets a true wilderness experience. Just below the tree line the mosquitoes are the size of helicopters, so don't forget the bug juice. Bring excellent walking shoes, extra food and a first aid kit (especially elastic bandages for sprained ankles). Once you hit the higher elevations, you are truly on your own. But try to limit your pack to twenty five to thirty pounds. You will curse every pound you carry. One reason that you want to travel light is that oxygen is hard to come by up there. My unacclimatized cardiovascular system produced a pounding pulse rate of a hundred and fifty beats per minute as I began setting up my tent between two glacial lakes above the timber line. But whatever the hardships, the vistas you encounter will engrave themselves on your memory and become a treasure forever. This is not to be missed.

As the summer progressed and one small crisis after another came and went, friendships developed among the clinical staff. In my opinion, middle age is a very difficult time for priests and nuns. They begin to watch the core of life, i.e. intimacy, marriage, children and grandchildren etc. pass them by. The commuter train of fulfillment is pulling out of the station and they are still standing on the platform. You can argue that they have their religious communities to support them, but it's not the same. It's cruel in a way. In times of stress and crisis good men and women need each other.

As chance would have it, one of the priests and a nun felt a mutual attraction to each other. Of course they did what any healthy religiously committed couple would do. They gave into temptation. You could see them experiencing the same initial awkwardness that teenagers experience. It was kind of cute.

I shared an apartment with the involved priest. One night Fred came in quietly about 2.00 am. I decided to yank his chain and asked "Fred, what exactly is going on here?" Fred paused for a minute, turned toward me and said "Sam, you have to understand that we are pledged to poverty, chastity and obedience; and we figure that any two out of three at any one time is good enough." I was speechless. I had been told.

Towards the end of the summer there was a mass arrest of the picketing farm workers. I'm not sure what set off that arrest. The strike organizers continued to sing songs and chant slogans in their jail cells. A few days after the arrests, the police were able to pinpoint the strike leaders. Those leaders were then segregated from the rest of the farm workers and placed in a single cell. Late one evening the police turned their powerful fire hoses into that cell. After several minutes of knocking the farm workers over with the water from the fire hose, the police opened the cell door and waded into the farm workers swinging clubs.

The police knew that any wounds would heal by the time this all came to court. But there was one flaw in their plan. According to

California state law a sick or injured prisoner may request their own personal physician. The farm workers did just that.

John and I waited in a stark empty jail house room while the farm workers were brought in and out one at a time. The atmosphere was tense. The first farm worker hobbled into the room. In a voice filled with resolute emotion, he said "John, they beat us". This is not hearsay. I saw the bruises and welts myself. John quietly pulled a 35mm camera out of his doctor's bag and photographed each injury.

Toward the end of August, John got involved in the home care of a farm worker who had worked for and supported the farm worker's union for years. José was now in his seventies with diabetes and end stage kidney disease. Finally, he had to be hospitalized. While José was on his deathbed, John arranged for a special visit. Caesar Chavez came unannounced into José's hospital room, José had led a humble life, and to have the leader of a major Mexican American movement visit him was totally unexpected. I was not there, but reportedly José's face glowed like the sun. Soon afterwards, he died peacefully.

It was now time to head back to New York City. After a heartfelt goodbye from the clinic staff, I took the northern route home. All I remember about the trip was travelling across southern Minnesota. It is the land of ten thousand lakes, it is beautiful and it goes on forever.

The summer following my second year at Union turned out to be a bit more low key. I became the Medical Director of a Girl Scout Camp in upstate New York. A friend of mine was the camp's senior administrator and asked if I wanted the job. A nurse had to leave the camp part way through the summer session and they needed someone to fill in during the last six weeks. Well, why not? After all, I was still in a full right leg cast from my first skiing experience, so my prospects for employment were limited. It was also outdoors and I loved being outdoors. How hard could it be?

Working with the Girl Scouts was a bit less intense than working with the United Farm Workers. There was a slight lesbian buzz to some of the senior girl counselors, but it didn't seem to matter. The campers got excellent care. At the end of the summer there were many tears when it came time to go home. Many of the campers did not want to go home. For the first time, some of the girl scouts found people who would actually listen to them.

At the end of the summer one of the senior staff members had a birthday. We decided to throw a spontaneous off campus celebration. We got slightly tanked and returned to the camp about 1.00 am. We then went down to the lake front and had a game of naked tag in the pool where we taught the campers how to swim. It seemed like a good idea at the time. After all, what difference did it make? All the campers were asleep. Little did we know that, under a full moon, the campers were sitting on top of a cliff on the other side of the lake taking in the whole scene. Oops! Once again, much heat. I can just imagine the letters those campers sent home after that little event.

During the final year at Union a group of us liberated a turn of the century faculty apartment located in an old Manhattan brownstone. The apartment had five bedrooms, three bathrooms and a very comfortable living space. Can you imagine what that apartment, sold as a condominium, would be worth today?

Eight of us moved into the apartment. Friends were always coming and going. Involvement in the anti-war movement was intense. In addition we took in a young man who had terminal cancer. He came to New York City to be involved in a new clinical trial at the Sloan Kettering Hospital. As a result of that clinical trial, his cancer spontaneously remitted. Mel added his own wry humor to our situation. He opened a checking account at a local bank. Along with the usual "Welcome to our bank" paperwork, they gave him a pamphlet which contained the ten most common warning signs and symptoms of cancer. He said "I've already got it".

The focal point of that final year was dinner time. We sat around a large table that suffered from my lack of cooking skills. While eating, we threw ideas back and forth. These weren't your routine dinner time conversations. Every idea you put out was examined and challenged. Your thinking had to be clear; you had to show the math. This wasn't some academic exercise. This was us trying to get our values straight before we launched ourselves into the real world. It was great to be with people who demonstrated such creative and original thinking. For years afterwards I missed those dinnertime conversations. After seminary, dinnertime simply became a time to eat food. Something vital was missing.

During our last year at Union, members of a social activist group called "The Community For Creative Non Violence", had been arrested. The charge was plotting to kidnap Henry Kissinger?!?! At a local protest I saw a button that read "Today Kissinger, tomorrow the Easter bunny". We had some deep connections to that group so we joined about nine hundred people who showed up for their trial in Harrisburg, Pennsylvania. Toward the end of the trial things looked really grim for the defendants. One church donated a large hall where we gathered the night before the verdicts were announced. Speakers from the stage updated us on the day's events in court. Suddenly the curtains drew back and there was a really good live Rock 'n' Roll band. As the music fired up, clowns appeared. They threw loaves of bread into the audience. It was a true "Feast of Fools". We danced on the pews for hours. This experience taught me one of the most valuable lessons that I carried away from seminary. When things get really bad, throw a party. When everything looks really bleak, create life.

Union did provide me with one really fun experience. During our third year, we were required to give a ten minute verbal presentation to the Department of Speech and Drama. Just for the hell of it, I did a comedy sketch. The director of the department held his sides with laughter. This is good. There is nothing worse than presenting comedy and receiving only silence for your efforts. So the director arranged for me to attend a seminar on comedy at the Lee Stausberg Institute of Drama. In a way, that's absurd. You can't teach someone how to be funny. You're either funny or you're not. But night after night they paraded the great comedians in front of us. These guys were tough, coming to age just after Vaudeville. As a comedian of that era, you were either funny or you starved, which isn't funny.

Soupy Sales was just an upbeat nice guy. The first thing Henny Youngman said to us was "I'll pay you $5 for each new original joke you send me. Don't send me the old ones. Believe me I've heard them all". Alan King did give us some tips on timing simply by telling elaborate jokes. He told one true story about George Burns and Jack Benny that had us on the edge of our chairs in terms of humor. All we needed by the end of the joke was one nudge (the punch line) to push us into spasms of laughter. We had been set up. That kind of craftsmanship in story telling comes only from years of experience on the stage. He also told us how he had to adapt his whole routine to the British comedy scene. Upon arriving in London he watched British comedians mumble some incomprehensible lines (which they still do) and the audience fell about laughing. Desperate, Alan decided to become the angry American comedian. The British ate it up. Comedy is indeed sink or swim. You must listen and adapt to your audience.

The other interesting aspect of the course were the drama students themselves. To my knowledge I was the only student in that audience who was not studying drama. Simply put, the drama students are always on stage. Every move is a delightful effort to draw attention to themselves. We could sit down and analyze this behavior, but that would kill the fun. It was great entertainment.

Finally our time at Union came to an end and we went our diverse and separate ways. I didn't know what to do. I would have become a psychotherapist, but I found working with depressed people really depressing. At this point the most meaningful part of my day was doing the laundry. There were also bills to pay and my monthly educational payments from the U.S. Army (the G.I. bill) had just run out.

I found my mind wandering back to medicine, so I went to a local emergency medical services office and talked to the director about becoming an Emergency Medical Technician. E.M.T's are the folk who ride around in ambulances. In New York City in the 1970s that was not a low key job.

The director said "You have to take the entire hundred and twenty hour course, but your experience in the military has taught you most of the course content already. I have a suggestion. There is a brand new Physician's Assistant Program opening up in Brooklyn. They need P.A.s to work in city clinics. As you know the Physician's Assistant concept was originally developed to give former Army Corpsmen the chance to use their clinical experience in civilian life. The program is a very intense two years. The first year is all academic study. The second year is a series of clinical rotations designed to sharpen your skills. At the end of it all, you get a Bachelor of Science degree and are eligible to sit the Physician Assistant National Certifying exam. We're trying to get the first class together now. What do you say?"

What did I say?! I had just finished seven years of academic studies.

However, I was at that point qualified to be a very interesting taxi driver. That's the beauty of the humanities; lots of ideas, no actual skill. But I would have to spend the rest of the summer taking organic chemistry as a prerequisite for the P.A program. More books. My heart sank. I was already an academic burn out. I told him I would think about it.

I walked out of the building in a daze. After crossing a few streets, I found myself facing the largest psychiatric hospital in Brooklyn. I noticed a grassy area about one acre in size, surrounded by high fences, where they let the psychiatric in-patients get some exercise. Those in-patients were a sorry lot; they were all subdued by their anti-psychotic medications. As they walked, their arms did not swing back and forth, but instead just hung at their sides. For reasons I cannot explain, the gate leading to the patient's exercise area was ajar. I entered. The patients immediately recognized that I was an outsider. When I walked, my arms moved.

I strolled around the grounds for about half an hour. Fortunately, no one closed the gate. I felt that if I was going to make the completely insane decision to go back into academics, then an insane asylum would be the perfect place to make that decision.

Chapter II

ON ACADEMICS

Let's start with what seems like a reasonable question. What should a student expect out of a college education? It's appropriate to make that inquiry considering that college will consume a ton of money and four years of a student's life. In an attempt to answer that question, I am going to assert that the goal of a college education should be to enrich a student's mind and prepare him or her for life's challenges. An academic institution should therefore work to expose the student to a series of creative experiences that not only opens their minds to a much broader world, but also equips them with skills to avoid life's very real pitfalls. That doesn't seem like too much to ask from an institution of higher learning.

My primary thesis is that many colleges fail in this undertaking. As I see it, the primary shortcomings of higher education lie in two distinct areas. The first problem area is the college faculty. Obviously most of the faculty are college graduates. If they studied the humanities then their post graduate career options are somewhat limited. What, besides writing term papers, do they really know how to do? A college graduate can go into primary school education or perhaps join a business that will show them how to actually make a living. Seeing these somewhat limited possibilities, many college graduates enter a Masters program. Once again that might better prepare them for business or teaching. Some go even further and enter a Doctoral program. They then drag themselves through years of research and the painstaking process of putting together a doctoral dissertation. Finally they graduate with the ultimate degree. But what does that ultimate degree actually prepare them to do? How many people on the planet really care about the content of that Doctoral thesis?

Having come through all of that class work, however, professors to be are now masters of the academic game. They are professional hoop jumpers. So, equipped with that skill, many graduates go back and teach at the college level. But having lived in the protected environment of multiple academic institutions, what do they actually know about the challenges life presents? The answer is: next to nothing. Sure they are well qualified to lead students through the test taking and paper writing exercises. But through all of this "education" many teachers never got their hands dirty. By and large, (and I admit this is a sweeping generalization) they have not immersed themselves in life's processes. So how can they realistically be expected to lead the young?

In my college there were two professors who were World War II veterans. Once in a while world events provide an unexpected agenda, and this hard reality was certainly true for both of them. The first professor spent his military career commanding a Navy destroyer. I spent most of my four years in college disagreeing with him. But I always had a feeling that he wasn't divorced from reality. Right or wrong, his opinions had context. He also showed real courage when cancer finally took him. He left behind a legacy of grateful students.

The second professor told us that while skiing down a Swiss mountain the weight of the machine gun on his back would literally pull him off the slope. He also had the privilege of being shot in the face by the Nazis. His life's experiences made this professor extremely pragmatic. The entire faculty followed his advice when it came to financial planning. He wasn't lost in the clouds.

I'm not suggesting that all faculty members enter a world war. But spending some time pumping gas, working as a volunteer in a mental institution, or as a big brother to a ghetto child might provide some grounding experiences. Even spending a summer walking the John Muir or Appalachian trails would help. The key point is for teachers to find meaningful life experiences before they try to lead students.

The second problem with colleges is the course curriculum. It may be interesting to learn what a rat will do in a maze, or how a group of people may respond to social stratification, or theorize on Plato's analogy of the cave, but how much of this will improve the quality of your day to day living? When I finally left college, I sat down and reviewed my classroom notes. I threw them all away. They were worthless. All of that time and money and I came away with a handful of good course experiences and some encounters with a few very creative people. That was it. The rest of it was a waste of time.

But rather than sit around and get bogged down in negative thinking, here are a few hopefully useful suggestions concerning possible college course curriculum content. First of all, how about a course that focuses on how to build a successful marriage? Greater than one third of all marriages end in divorce; therefore the cradle in which children are raised is often fragmented. So what can be taught in college to reduce the incidence of a painful divorce?

Spend the first six weeks of a course on marriage teaching people how to put together a responsible household budget. Make each student come up with a budget for a household of four on a fixed income. Then spend a lot of time showing the students how to avoid crippling credit card debt. Serious debt is a tremendous stressor in a marriage. Husband and wife start to blame each other for their situation. Much time is spent worrying about how the bills will be paid. Trust me, after graduation Visa, Master Card and American Express are all waiting with open arms and an A.P.R. greater than 18%. Do the math and show students what that A.P.R. actually amounts to over the years.

Speaking of fixed incomes, show students how to prepare for retirement. It's easy to ignore that oncoming reality, which will eventually result in the student being old, helpless and poor. Furthermore, spend some time on the option of renting an apartment versus buying a house. What are the tax implications? How much mortgage is too much mortgage?

After working through basic household economics, turn the course direction towards children's health. Review current childhood immunization protocols. What is the immunization schedule over the first five years of a child's life? What are the risks/benefits of those immunizations? What happens to a third world patient population where those immunizations are not given?

Then turn the focus towards a family's nutritional status. What does a newborn really need to eat, as opposed to all the new baby hype? What are the milestones of a normal child's growth and development? This is important because the earlier congenital problems are addressed, usually the better the outcome. Spend some additional time clarifying what constitutes a healthy adult diet. Show the relation between excessive fatty diets, cigarette smoking and heart and lung disease. Show the actual statistics and increased mortality that result from these self destructive life styles.

What are the basic skills a new mother needs to know? She and the new baby are brought home from the hospital with the mother physically and emotionally exhausted. All of the neighbors stop by and say "Oh how cute!" and run away at the first whiff of a dirty diaper. Mom is then left alone trying to cope with her colicky bundle of joy. Everyone thinks that when mom and baby get home from the hospital that "nature will take its course". What a load of rubbish! The average first time mom, unless she came from a large family, doesn't know squat about child rearing. The new mother often feels inadequate and overwhelmed. Post partum depression is a huge problem. It might be nice to give some insights into those issues before they happen.

Often if grandma is not there to step in and lend a hand, real trouble can develop in terms of the new mother decompensating and abusing the child. Even a bigger problem is the live in boyfriend who is not the child's father. He gets jealous of all the attention the baby gets, plus he can't sleep due to the child's unrelenting crying. The result is another case of "shaken baby syndrome" and resulting permanent brain damage being brought into the emergency room.

Raising children can be one of life's greatest experiences, but it's hard work and not for the faint of heart. Not infrequently the genetic dice will roll snake eyes and a child is born with lifelong health problems. Those problems can drain all the parent's emotional and financial resources. Sometimes the brain damage is so profound that the parents wonder (rightfully so) what was the point of them having a child in the first place? What are the odds of another disaster if the couple tries to have a second baby? Young people need this information.

As a reasonable alternative, expose students to the serious obstacles presented by the process of adopting a child. What challenges are presented if you want to adopt a third world child?

Simply put, the more educated young people are prior to becoming parents the better. The idea is not to scare them, but to inform them that this is really serious business. Just helping a young woman understand the physical adjustments her body will go through during pregnancy is worth the effort.

There is no excuse for new parents not knowing the obstructed airway sequence. In other words you need to know how to get the marble or the peanut out of your child's throat. I have at least two patients who are alive because their care givers had mastered this simple skill. Most parents think, well, odds are it won't happen to my child. That may be true. But can you imagine watching your child choke to death because you didn't know what to do? Once the airway is completely occluded, brain death starts in six minutes and is complete by ten minutes. Just waiting for the ambulance won't solve the problem.

The obstructed airway sequence is well presented in C.P.R. courses taught by instructors from your local hospital or Red Cross. Bring these professionals into the classroom. They will also let you practice these critical maneuvers on baby manikins. Without these skills, you are not an adequate parent.

New mothers often bring their babies to the emergency room far more often than necessary. Their actions are motivated by fear because they know little or nothing about their new baby's health care. Conversely their ignorance sometimes leads them to *not* bring their baby to the E.R when the baby is actually critically ill. Each local community health service will have a qualified team that teaches pediatric advanced life support (P.A.L.S.) courses. Why not invite these people into the classroom? The P.A.L.S.'s team will have a Power Point presentation to teach students how to recognize a really sick child. Unlike most healthy adults, young children can get very ill very quickly. The trick is to know the physical signs of an acute childhood illness. It's really not all that difficult. Just show the students slide after slide of seriously ill children and sprinkle the presentation with a bit of common sense. That's all it takes. The goal is not to turn every new parent into an expert pediatric health care provider at home. Instead the goal is to make a useful introduction to childhood emergency health issues. Even basic knowledge in this area is a quantum leap over parents who are helpless in a crisis.

Furthermore, what do you do if your child falls from a height, or jams a screwdriver into his wrist while trying to pry something open and starts to bleed profusely, or puts his arm through a plate glass window? Again the actual skills involved in the initial treatment of these problems are not complicated. You just have to know what to do. After the injury has occurred, there is no time for research.

Getting back to marriage, bring some seasoned marriage counselors into the classroom. Have them present and discuss the most frequent marital problems they see. For example, how do you deal with the sense of betrayal felt when your spouse is sexually unfaithful? Half of all marriages go through this difficult and painful trauma. What factors lead to the affair in the first place? This has to be followed by two weeks on the basics of sexually transmitted diseases. The students need to know what blood tests they will need over what period of time after their spouse confesses infidelity.

What do you do when your in-laws won't let you lead your own life? Where do you go for help? What if you're financially dependent on them, and they feel they have a right to call the shots in your life?

How do you deal with spousal abuse? This is a common problem. Are your children in danger? What are the real options?

What happens when you find out you have married an alcoholic or drug addict? What affect is their addiction having on you? Were you raised in a similar environment? These are extremely serious issues.

Oh oh! Your company consolidated and eliminated your job. Now what? However, the bank has been calling your wife for months. They want her to work full time in their accounting department. They aren't offering her a lot of money, but the benefits package is solid. If your wife goes to work full time, could you step up to the plate at home? How about a course on cooking for men only? If you're living on your wife's income you can't afford restaurants five nights a week. The food offered at the fast food joints is full of calories, salt and fat. Do you want your kids to develop a taste for that crap? So it's you, the kids and the kitchen. Will you know what to do? Or are you going to open the same tin of ravioli night after night until your children rise up as one and slay you?

Have you ever heard of the Myth of Sisyphus? It's where a mortal pisses off a god. As a general rule, it's never a good idea to piss off a god or a possessed person. When their eyes glow orange, it's time to back off. As a punishment, Sisyphus has to spend his whole day pushing a large boulder up the side of a hill. When he finally gets to the top, he must stand to one side and watch the rock roll all the way back down to the bottom of the hill. Then he has to start pushing the rock up the hill all over again. He has to repeat this process every day for eternity. This is exactly what daily housework is like. The laundry never stops. You clean up from one meal and it's time to start thinking about the next. The cat just vomited on the rug. The bathroom looks like it belongs in a bus station. You spend all morning sweeping, washing and waxing the kitchen floor. Then three kids with mud soaked boots burst through the kitchen door. On the television commercial for the kitchen floor cleaner, the mother just smiles, kisses the kids and effortlessly mops up the mess. In real life, the mother's eyes glow orange.

Whatever you do, get that housework bound spouse out of the house several times a week and give them something to smile about. If the kids turn out to be solid human beings, it will be because of that spouse's hard work. Do not *ever* take house spouse's efforts for granted. That alone can sour a marriage.

My college required four semesters of a foreign language. Foreign language study does expand one's awareness of the world, but you still spend much of your time locked up in the language lab stuffing your face with Doritos while you memorize vocabulary lists. In addition to studying the language, how about requiring spending a semester (or summer) in a third world community project? Spending a much shorter time in a similar mission project convinced me to go to medical school. (By the way, never go on a mission project where the locals are kidnapping or killing. That danger is very real and you don't need it).

Give the students at the community project real responsibility. Let them know that the new roof has to be on the orphanage prior to the upcoming monsoon season. If they fail, the orphans get wet.

Let college students watch the locals struggle for items of food, clothing and shelter that the students have taken for granted every day since they were born. The impact of an experience like this will change a student forever. Also, working directly with third world people might ignite a lifelong fire in a student's soul. Classroom work alone rarely has that effect.

Although studying a foreign language is a good idea, you may never use it. In addition to a foreign language, require students to take two semesters of information technology. Without computer skills, a young person cannot compete in today's job market.

Require the Speech and Drama department to prepare each student for job interviews. Have the students do mock interviews in front of a camera. You could learn a great deal by watching yourself on a video. Maybe that facial tattoo was a mistake after all.

To sum up, why not put a third of college course curriculum under a department entitled "Life Skills"? There can be no sacred cows. Marriage, human sexuality, child rearing etc. etc., all have to fall under intense scrutiny and debate. But there is an additional issue here. Remember my primary thesis that "Everyone is flipping nuts"? Purely academic pursuits allow people to largely avoid their own craziness because it's all a sterile cerebral exercise. But when people debate subjects as personal as the ones mentioned above, people's neurotic thinking emerges. The earlier in life that you confront your own craziness the better your life will be.

These are a few of the many creative ideas that can be incorporated into a college curriculum. It's important to realize that higher learning is not a static process. As our understanding of what students actually need evolves, higher education has to be flexible enough to steer course content in both a useful and pragmatic direction.

I can hear college professors argue that the above mentioned subjects are not really academic in nature. That may be true. But these subjects are certainly relevant, useful and good value for money. It all depends on what you want to have when you walk away with your diploma. We need to construct curriculums that will engender in students a genuine sense of gratitude when they graduate.

In conclusion, do we care enough about our children to allow them to openly confront life's challenges? Or are we going to send them, without a road map, into a world full of quicksand?

Chapter III

HOW ONE LARGE SKUNK CAN CHANGE YOUR LIFE

After college I drove through the western United States to get some fresh air between my ears. I desperately needed a change from the sterility of academia.

As a child I was always interested in caverns. That interest led me down the Texas panhandle on my way to Carlsbad Caverns in New Mexico. Just outside of Lubbock it was time to stop for the night. Usually I would pitch my small tent to save money. But a strong gut feeling told me to find shelter for the night. In the far distance to the west I noticed a small thick dark cloud with an eerie orange color at its center. It was just before sunset and I remember thinking "That's unusual". I pulled into a small generic motel. As I drove into a parking space, I became aware that my car would be out in the open. Another gut feeling made me move the car and park instead under a protected part of the motel.

After getting my room key, I ate a quick bite and settled in. Then the wind started. I was surprised because when dusk came there was no sign of any big storm. Suddenly it was dark and the rain turned to hail. The wind became so powerful that the windows by my bed were shaking. I ended up sitting in the corner furthest away from the windows to avoid broken glass.

Early the next morning I walked outside and across the debris. My motel had lost thirty two windows. The motel across the street lost its roof. The open parking space where I had originally parked my car turned out to be the landing pad for a Coca Cola vending machine. The Ford that eventually parked there did not do well. After I paid up, the old man who ran the motel said "Son, you have to understand that when the wind gets going out here, there's just not much to stop it". Had I pitched my pup tent out in that tornado, this might have been a much shorter book, or no book at all.

Carlsbad Caverns was not a disappointment. In a cavern in the eastern United States, a limestone room as big as a house is considered large. There is a room in Carlsbad Caverns that is a mile in circumference. Some of the ornate detail in the limestone formations defies belief. The entrance to the caverns sits on a high plateau. I found myself wondering how the river that formed the caverns could be located in such an elevated but flat area. Most rivers run in a valley. As it turns out, Carlsbad Caverns is so old that the mountains that surrounded the entrance and held the river in place have all disappeared. We are talking about a time span of well over one hundred million years.

From Carlsbad, I continued my journey through all the major national parks of the Great South West. What an invigorating time. I finished up with the Grand Canyon. Standing on the edge of the south rim, the mind's eye cannot take in a ditch that size. It's just too big. I put together an overnight pack and walked to the bottom of the canyon in order to appreciate what my eyes could not initially interpret. Near the bottom, I met a fun young couple and we walked together for a while. Soon we were hiking through a long pedestrian tunnel carved out of solid rock. It was cool in the tunnel; but when we exited at the far end, we were suddenly in 104 degree Fahrenheit heat. The girl fainted. Her companion scooped her up and carried her back into the tunnel. She recovered quickly, put the back of her forearm to her forehead and said "Oh Ralph, you really *do* love me!" It was great theater.

At the very bottom of the Grand Canyon lies a dude ranch. Inside that ranch sits a swimming pool. After walking for hours in that heat, there was no way to keep anyone out of that swimming pool. We never broke stride. We just dropped our back packs and walked straight into the pool. Afterwards we paid an enormous amount of money for a sandwich and a soda. Where else could you go for cheaper food? The next closest restaurant was a six hour hike straight up.

From Arizona I headed for the Grand Tetons. Coming into the Tetons, I found myself driving on a reasonably flat and heavily forested plateau. The scenery was relatively unchanging. Then I drove around a corner and the Tetons stood before me. Take the Grand Canyon, double its depth, turn it upside down and you have the Tetons. It was one of those sights that stays with you forever. I found a camp site and settled in for the night. After pitching my tent, I went back to my parked car. I needed to look at some maps to see where I could safely hike into the Tetons with minimal bad weather equipment. After scanning the maps I headed back to the tent. Standing in front of my tent was a skunk about the size of a spare tire. This animal was half skunk and half Godzilla. He turned his head to stare at me. His beady black eyes betrayed an intense irritation. He was packing some serious heat and he knew it. I thought "This might be a good time to call home." I had not talked to Mom or Dad for about six weeks, but when you are twenty two years old you don't think about that stuff. Fortunately there was a pay phone at the camp site.

I expected a warm hello from my father. Instead, his first words were "Where the hell have you been?! You've been drafted!" Oh oh! Reality check! I guess the Canadian Rockies will have to wait. The next morning, sans skunk, I turned the car back towards home.

Now I was faced with a huge dilemma that I knew sooner or later would become unavoidable. I had been drafted into the military and was soon going to be ordered to kill people I had never met. Think about that. You take ordinary young men and turn them into killers. Ethical issues to one side, this has to be one of life's strangest twists.

The critical issue in my mind centered on whether or not there was enough justification for me to kill strangers. I am not a pacifist. Some people are so evil they need to be killed. But historical events were now forcing me to examine the roots of the Vietnam War.

The key to understanding any war lies in the history of the cultures in question. If you want to really understand what's going on, you must start a few thousand years prior to the current conflict and work your way forward. Every war has a historical context and the importance of that context cannot be over emphasized. That's why we may have failed in Iraq. We had no real understanding of the tribal culture and traditions surrounding Sadam Hussein when we went in with "Shock and Awe". By the time we really went to school on Iraq's culture, the horse was truly out of the barn. Catch up baseball can be a difficult game to play.

But back in 1969, all I knew about Iraq was that it sat somewhere between the U.S.A and India. However in 1969 everyone knew the location of Vietnam as we became drawn deeper and deeper into that painful conflict. The United States' official White Paper on Vietnam argued that the communist presence in Vietnam was threatening to eventually topple the countries of South East Asia like a series of dominos. The Catholic Church argued that its missions in South East Asia were under assault by the communists. Khrushchev had been banging his shoe on his United Nations desk saying "We will bury you!" The horrible truth is that there was no way that the cold war was not going to be slugged out in that small South East Asian country. The conflict was unavoidable; historical forces and cultures were on a collision course.

Ho Chi Min had decided that Vietnam was no longer going to be a French colonial power. Initially he was friendly to the United States, saving downed American pilots in World War II. Early on in the revolution he petitioned the United States for support, but there was no way the United States was going to back a regime that was fighting France right after World War II. Ho Chi Min realized that his only source of help were the Communist countries.

In 1946 the first of the two Indo Chinese wars began. The French fought hard in both wars, but they were strangers in a strange land and got their butts kicked. Much international political effort resulted in a cease fire in 1954. Vietnam ended up partitioned into two halves, the north and the south. Communist sympathizers were to move north, while colonialists headed south. After a two year cooling off period, a national election was to be held to decide who would govern Vietnam. Polls done by the West showed that in any democratic election Ho Chi Min would have won by as much as an eighty percent majority. But these were the years of "better dead than red", so the United States cancelled the democratic election and set up a corrupt puppet regime in South Vietnam. Madam Nhu, South Vietnam's new first lady decided that she was going to change the citizens of a traditionally Buddhist country into Catholics. How stupid can you get? In response, Buddhist monks began to protest the suppression of their religion by setting themselves on fire. These and other polarizing events set the stage for war.

As the Vietnam War intensified, the violence became unrelenting. During that war more bombs were dropped on South East Asia than fell in all of World War II. In the secret war in Laos and Cambodia alone, one bomb was dropped an average of every nine minutes for eight years.

I was asked to become a very small pawn in this apocalypse. I decided that the justification for me to become a killer was just not there.

The domino theory could have been correct, but history showed that the Vietnamese and Chinese had been fighting each other for two thousand years. The idea that all of the South East Asian cultures would become absorbed into one Communist bloc like Eastern Europe seemed possible, but unlikely.

My political activism first began when I saw a photograph of Vietnamese civilians who had been struck by napalm. I was moved to tears. Soon afterwards I initiated a local fundraiser for medical supplies for North Vietnamese civilians caught up in the war. The money we raised went directly to the Quaker church. The medical supplies were then delivered to the Quaker's counterparts in the Buddhist Church in Vietnam. The monks then delivered the aid to civilians.

All of this led me to declare myself a conscientious objector to the Vietnam War. However, this presented a problem. In those days you could not apply for conscientious objector status based on the dictates of your own individual conscience. You could only become a conscientious objector if your church told you not to kill. If you think about that, it's crazy. How in the world do you separate religious beliefs from issues involving individual conscience? Welcome to Catch 22.

Conscientious Objector status at that point in history was just the military's way of getting the organized church off its back. Therefore I needed an organized church to stand behind me. But I was Presbyterian, not exactly a pacifist branch of Christianity. If you visit Scotland, which is the birth place of the Presbyterian denomination, their churches are full of war memorials. To the Scots, their Christian faith and their valor in war are inseparable. I knew this was going to be a hard sell.

I petitioned my local church leadership for help. A meeting was held involving our pastor, elders, deacons and me. I pleaded my case for C.O. status. Some of the church elders were World War II veterans. To them, burning a draft card was on a par with committing rape. I was thrown out of the room and a heated debate followed. Finally they decided unanimously to stand behind me. They wrote a letter of support to my draft board. Had they not backed me up, I would have been faced with an interesting choice:

No.1   Canada
No.2   Jail

Fortunately, because of my home church's loyalty, I never had to make that choice.

There are two types of conscientious objectors. "1 – O" will have nothing to do with the military and alternative services are found for those individuals. The second category of conscientious objector is the 1 – A – O. That individual will serve in the military, but will not bear arms. Those objectors are shipped en masse to Fort Sam Houston in Texas to become combat medics. For me this was the beginning of a life long career.

At this point allow me to offer a suggestion to future conscientious objectors. You must get your C.O. status clarified *before* you join the military. After you take the oath during the swearing in ceremony, the military owns you. It is extremely difficult at that point to turn around and say "I've changed my mind! I don't want to play soldier!" If you do that the military will call you a coward and make you pay big time. Therefore in order to save yourself a world of grief, get your C.O. status confirmed *in writing* long before you have all the hair shaved off your head.

Although my decision to become a conscientious objector turned out to be one of the best decisions I ever made, it was also one of the most difficult. All through the decision making process I was plagued by doubt. What if I was wrong? What if the domino theory was true? The Russians had already tried to put nuclear missiles in Cuba. Was I actually helping Communist aggression? Nowadays the answers to these questions are not hard to find. But back then, the issues were anything but clear. I learned from this experience that, once in a while, major life decisions have to be made without adequate information to make sure that you are right. Sometimes you have to go with the best information you have at the time, be as honest as possible, make the decision and live with the consequences. Making this decision marked the beginning of my stepping out of a protected academic environment and dealing with the real world.

But there is another side to this story. Although my C.O. status stood in direct opposition to the military's goals, I have to say that while I was in the Army I never received one bad word as a result of my being a conscientious objector. That lack of criticism was partially a result of my receiving a lot of extra medical training prior to my being shipped to

Vietnam. My first duty station was located in Virginia Beach, Virginia. If you are going to defend the country, do it at Virginia Beach. The doctors we worked with preferred not to be dragged out of bed in the middle of the night to see each patient. Therefore they trained their medics to handle basic night time emergencies. We were like a small family in our little clinic. But the medical experience I gained in a year at Virginia Beach was worth its weight in gold in the Vietnam jungle. I took good care of the troops and they watched out for me.

The fact that I never took any flack for being a conscientious objector filled me with certain gratitude. I knew that in many countries, someone who took a C.O. stance would be quickly put up against the wall, shot, buried and forgotten. We do have a lot to be grateful for in the United States.

But having said that, I cannot imagine anyone who finds themselves in a combat situation not having the insight to see that brave young men killing each other is the depth of insanity. Obviously the first order of business in war is to simply survive. But when the shooting finally stops, the combat soldier will never be the same again. War has gone on since the beginning of time and will never stop, but what a negative and overwhelmingly cruel thing to do.

Finally, in order to be ethically consistent I should have chosen 1 – 0 conscientious objector status. After all, if you are serving in the military you are to some degree helping the war effort. But a part of me wanted to see what war was all about. I also had a strong feeling that I was not going to die. As a result of a lot of historical forces and my own convictions I entered the fire storm in 1971. I must have been crazy.

After I returned from Vietnam I wrote about my war time experiences. It was a way of purging my fears and starting over. These experiences will speak for themselves in the following pages, which were written in 1974.

i

Chu Lai

We had just entered the republic of Vietnam. Apprehensions were understandably high. Rumors. Last week a rocket had just missed the camp and fallen into the sea.

There were signs up with the symbols and patches of the various units we would be joining. They were as obscure to us as the battery of numbers on our orders that carried our fate.

Explosions. Mines and booby traps. They spent a lot of time showing us how to spot the enemy's booby traps while at the same time teaching us to construct our own. The Geneva Convention prohibits "booby traps", so we called them "mechanical ambushes". Double speak. Explosions, mines, explosions, bear traps, explosions, det cord, chi coms, bamboo stakes, grenade launchers, war stories. Explosions of fear, crumbling of consciousness. "Thou shalt not kill"! We lost that very quickly. Gooks, slits, V.C, Charley (lately Sir Charles), any element of speech that identified our targets as human was swiftly removed. The enemy was only known as a threat to our existence. We were bad mother fuckers. That's what we wanted to be. Everyone carried a bag of their own aspirations, the primary one being to return home alive.

I learned to fire the M16. "Just in case," I told myself. As a C.O. I resented being so defenseless. I wanted to live. I was afraid. It's easy to be non violent in college. It's something else to be against violence in the midst of violence. We were being prepared to kill. It was so easy. I'll never forget how smoothly that preparation went. The guys ate it up. The tide almost literally swept us away. Many of us were going to be killed by those going through the same preparation on the other side. But no one seemed to challenge our being placed in this position.

I walked near the beach late in the evening. I felt like I was the last sane man on earth. I had no community, no shared vision or concern. I was truly alone.

It's so hard to do something different, especially when you are by yourself and everyone else is moving with the tide. That was the loneliest I've ever been.

Two days later I located a close friend. We had gone through C.O. training together. He had entered Vietnam prior to my arrival and gotten a rear job. We spent an evening together just before I left for the "bush". Don showed me the opening chapter of a book he was writing. It was on human nature and how humankind was reaping back the violence that had been poured out on the earth. I can't remember the specifics of what he wrote. I do remember the feeling that it was one of the most sensitive and perceptive expositions about humankind I had ever read. It corresponded so closely to my own experience. I was no longer alone.

We sat around our instructor as he showed us the finer points of a Claymore mine. "Learn how to aim this thing!" He said. He continued with an illustration; "In the unit I was with, we set up a "mechanical ambush" along the trail. We saw three N.V.As. (North Vietnamese Army Soldiers) hike down the trail, hit the trip wire, and we watched the mine explode. But you know what we found when we went down to the trail? Not three dead dinks. We found three pairs of boots with feet in them. Whoever had set up the mine had not sighted it properly and the blast was too low. The N.V.A had crawled off into the undergrowth and it cost us three wounded G.Is. before we could finish those mother fuckers off. So men, you've got to learn to aim those Claymores."

Firebase Maryann

I stood at the edge of the perimeter looking down at the quiet jungle and the shallow swift river running below. No civilization for miles. What a beautiful country. I had just stepped off the helicopter from Chu Lai. I was "new meat." Thump! whistle. I ducked instinctively. I had never heard a mortar fire. I watched in fascination as a puff of smoke appeared down by the river followed a half second later by a fragmenting "crunch". "Let's try a "human eliminator"… The voice came drifting over from the mortar crew. Thump! whistle. It was like the 4th of July. This mortar crew had four days to live. After watching several more rounds, I decided to amble back toward the aid station. I passed the Communication (or "Commo") shack and noticed the blond fellow with glasses walking out. He too had four days to live.

About this time, Alpha Company whom I was soon to join, got a kill. Whoever pulled the trigger was rewarded with a three day pass. Two days later the same company returned to where the "kill" had taken place. The body was gone. Instead they found a note on a stick. The note said in Vietnamese "they killed Taun! Now we get together and kill lots of G.Is".

Up by the aid station Captain Morris was addressing Charley Company. Captain Morris had lost his balls on his first trip to Vietnam. He was back for revenge. He too was doomed.

The next day my attack of the flu improved enough to let me go out to my first field assignment. If my flu had not improved, I would be dead.

I packed three days of heavy canned rations plus all my medical gear into my rucksack and caught the next supply helicopter out. After a short ride we began spiraling like a cork screw entering a bottle. Sitting on the door of the chopper, I was looking directly down at the ground as we spiraled. We landed and I jumped off into knee deep fallen foliage. While bare backed men quickly unloaded the supplies (a stationary chopper is a sitting duck) I asked for Doc Williams.

Word got around that I was looking for him and he came up from the tree line to greet me. I shook his hand. "Hi, I'm Sam Davisson I'm your replacement." His face lit up like a Christmas tree.

It was late afternoon, so I began to set up for the night. Everything stopped after dark. I tied up my hammock with boot strings after clearing out a small space between two trees. I noticed that everyone was swinging low to the ground. But I figured out that the ground is where the creatures are so I tied my hammock about four feet off the ground. I also tied a Poncho overhead as a makeshift roof as I had been told to do. Darkness came and I made an attempt at sleeping bent up in a hammock. After about an hour it started to rain. Someone took the trouble to tie the head portion of the poncho shut for me, but they forgot to tell me to put the head portion on the outside of my roof instead of the inside. Gradually it filled up with water until it looked like a grapefruit. Then it burst. "Oh fuck!" As I was struggling in the hammock, the boot strings broke. I learned why people swung close to the ground. As I lay on the ground muttering to myself and blowing up my air mattress, I felt something on my leg. I had never felt it before, but I knew what it was. I had a leech. I had to use my flash light to find my bug juice to get him off. I did so and a small stream of blood ran down my leg. The night watch found me and explained very politely "Doc you can't shine your light at night." Translation; "Doc you could get us all killed."

Two days and miles of "humping" later, the news came over our radio. Maryann was hit and overrun. N.V.A. sappers came in under the cover of their own mortar shells and hurled satchel charges into the bunkers. They knew where everything was, T.O.C., the Commo shack, etc. etc…

A week later I returned to Maryann. It had been rebuilt and the important positions had been shifted around. That should fool the enemy for at least a couple of days. I talked to Doc Howard. He was a man of solid character that everybody liked. He was Charlie Company's medic and had been in the rear the night of the disaster. I listened as he told me in detail how his friends had died. Specific names and faces came alive for a brief moment and then died violently. He got this information by talking with survivors. For the first time I experienced that human beings are behind the numbers of dead and wounded that Walter Cronkite announced every night on the evening news. But the real story for me was Doc Howard. He was shattered.

Walking back to the aid station, I saw one of the many small dogs that populated the fire base. He was trotting with something in his mouth. Back home *it might have been a bone or a stick. I looked closely. It was a human foot. I was horrified, but in an almost grotesquely cynical way. I was both detached and bitter at the same time.*

iv

For years in college I had awakened to a buzzing alarm clock. This morning I woke up to the long drawn out blast of a Claymore mine. I was startled for a moment. It was still dark. Sometimes an animal would set these things off. Apprehensive silence. Then Dean opened up with his "pig" (M.60 machine gun). Everybody in my section of the platoon grabbed their weapon and waited. I rolled from my hammock, strapped my bandage bags into place and threw on my boots. Waiting. More machine gun fire. I became concerned about what was going on, so I worked my way to the end of the perimeter where the fire had originally come from. A few of the guys were crouched down behind vegetation. We had camped in the middle of an N.V.A. trail. I looked down the trail where Dean, the Commanding Officer and several men had disappeared. I asked "Do you think they need a medic?" Of course Mark had no way of knowing. The first rays of dawn were creeping up across the sky. He replied "Maybe you should go down and see". I agreed. I started off down the trail alone. Now I was really apprehensive. I didn't have to go far before I came across Captain Harley bending over a half naked Vietcong. Apparently this VC had disconnected the trip wire and battery and picked up the Claymore mine that protected our perimeter at night. What incredible courage. But because we were camped on a trail, someone had taken the extra precaution of putting out a second mine. The man lying before me never saw it. He was very young. God help us if he had got inside of our perimeter with his AK47. We were all asleep except for a guard on the other side of the perimeter.

The second mine was defective and had not caught the man who was now my patient in a direct blast. Consequently he was not shredded, but the whole upper portion of his body was covered with small scratches from dirt and rocks thrown by the explosion. One of those scratches was killing him. His eyes were wide open, full of dirt and seeing nothing. I knew he was in deep trouble but I couldn't see why. Captain Harley couldn't either. It was still pretty dark. My mind was still foggy. Captain Harley rejoined his troops pursuing the other

54

V.C.s. "Where's the wound?!?" Nothing but scratches. Eyes staring. Nothing. A gasping breath. My only clue. I sat there for a few minutes, bewildered and helpless. "Where's the fucking wound?!" One more gasping breath. Then for the first time when his chest had fully expanded I heard a gurgling sound from one of the scratches. "Oh Jesus!" One of the tiny pellets from the mine not much bigger than a B.B. had pierced his left lung, at least. I had an emergency bag and pulled Vaseline gauze from it, the most airtight bandage I had. I then re-enforced it with several layers of elastic bandage leaving one end of the dressing open to prevent a tension pnumothorax. He stopped breathing. I pulled out a breathing tube and began to breath for him. His chest was rising so I knew I was getting air into him. My assistant, an infantry man who had some first aid training in the States came out to join me. I had given him further training and supplied him with everything but drugs. "Pops, sucking chest wound! Reinforced the bandage!" I continued the breathing. The patient's heartbeat stopped a minute later. "Pops his heart stopped! Heart massage and breathing, ready, count 1 – 5, start!" We worked at him for five minutes. I had never seen Pops work in an emergency. He was great. I was proud of him. After a few more minutes though, I felt our patient grow cold and stiff in my arms, slowly like a wave going over his body. He was dead.

I had a perfectly normal lunch. No tears or emotion. I began to wonder about myself as a human being. I began to understand that you can't feel and at the same time perform in the situations the Army put you in. Upon realizing that, I began to understand the evil present in war, that human beings have to switch to "off" in order to function.

Wham! We looked back from our position on the hillside down to the valley where one of our platoons was working. One of our point men, Victor, had just lost both his legs and his balls in a booby trap. The old Sergeant we called "John Wayne" bandaged Victor's wounds while keeping the other men out of sight. He muttered to himself, "If they see this, I'll never get another man to walk point."

We gathered around "Screw" Genes's radio and listened to the tragedy play by play. The Lieutenant screamed over the radio, "I need a dust-off!" Captain Harley tried to calm him down. From that point on I never let a group go more than a hundred yards away from the main body without a medic or somebody we had trained. Victor flashed the peace sign as the medivac chopper carried him away.

vi

"Doc, I got my first dink last night!" Henry stood there grinning like a child who had just learned to tie his shoes. With as much sarcasm as I could muster, I answered: "Congratulations".

"Where's the smoke?"

"I don't see it!"

"There it is!" A red plume began to billow up from an entirely green landscape. We were huddled like anxious parents watching our children's little league game. "Waited until too late in the morning to bring in the Claymore", somebody mumbled in the background. "A sniper was waiting for him when he went out to get it."

From our elevated position on a hilltop stripped bare of anything living, we watched a loach helicopter circle like a dragonfly over a red rose finally to be engulfed by the green. But only for a second. Quickly the dragonfly rose again. It moved towards us in a way that let us know that our part in one tiny segment of a long, sad story was about to begin.

"Sam, you take his head!" L.T. quickly gave orders to others. In a few seconds the dragonfly dropped its gift into our arms. A young G.I was pulled from the door gunners lap. His eyes saw nothing. We carried him in to the aid station shack. In my hands the hastily wrapped bandage originally placed around his head by the field medic fell off. It looked like a farmer's plough had gone up at the back of his head. We laid him in our emergency cot and began our work. He might have been eighteen.

"Ace wraps! Ace wraps!"

The breathing tube... how does it?... doesn't it go...? I grabbed the tube from Doc Glenfield and put it into the boy soldier's mouth. L.T. started to breathe for him as I began rebandaging his head. The bandage in place, L.T. ran out of breath. I took over. "Can't get any pressure!" I gasped. L.T. clasped both his hands on the victim's lips.

"Hey, this guy's been shot in the foot"! "Harder!" The fellow doing the heart massage wasn't pushing hard enough. In my panic I shouted orders to him.

"Harder, dammit, use the base of your hand." Gurgling sounds. The eyes *looking into nothingness.*

"Harder! Break his ribs if you have to! That's it!"

I knew somewhere in the back of my mind that our breathing and heartbeat sequence was wrong, but somehow it didn't seem too important at the time.

After about fifteen minutes of our desperate efforts, word came that a helicopter was ready to take him to the rear. Continuing our mouth to mouth breathing we carried him to the chopper. L.T. motioned to the dust off medic to continue breathing for him. The medic looked puzzled. L.T. jumped in and took over. "He's not dead until a doctor tells me he's dead," L.T. muttered. It was a euphemism we learned in our medical training. I knew that the time he had not been breathed for between the red smoke and firebase had been too long.

Back in the rear as he was being taken into surgery, my bandage fell off and half his brains fell out on the floor. The surgeon just looked at L.T. and shook his head.

Meanwhile, I was lost. His dog tags indicated that he was Latin American (a Spanish name). I thought of the two fellows from Puerto Rico who went through basic training with me. They barely knew what was going on. No chance of rank for them. They were in a foreign war, dragged from their native land into a conflict they knew nothing about. They barely spoke English. They believed in the Bible, the words of Jesus, which is why they were training as C.O's with me. I guess I'm trying to say they were innocent. I felt the same way about our patient.

I walked around afterwards wanting to share something. Part of me wanted to share that I had been involved in something important. But there was something else. Maybe screaming sorrow. I didn't know. Still a great distance between my role and my feelings. I found one of our guys and related the story to him. He said "Yeh, I can see his blood on your T-shirt." I looked down. I hadn't even noticed.

Our new Forward Observer had just joined our company in the jungle. He was a young sergeant right out of school. Every company had a Forward Observer. His job was to call in the artillery and illumination rounds that would protect our perimeter during an attack.

Our previous Forward Observer was on a Pan Am flight home having finished his tour of duty. He was a real ace in the deck, a young lieutenant and a feisty Texas boy with an almost photographic memory. He was also an ace in the deck for another reason. Because he was one of four people in the entire company who knew how to play bridge, whenever a typhoon would pin us down the cards would come out. What bothered me a bit is that he would call in precautionary artillery rounds during the bidding. I prayed that he wouldn't get the bidding numbers mixed up with the artillery coordinates, but he never did. He would radio in a battery of six "Horny Elephants" (high explosive) rounds, and without pausing ask "What's trump?"

On the other hand, our new Forward Observer was anxious to show us what he could do. While we were taking a lunch break from our "humping" (walking through a steamy jungle with a full pack), he started calling in coordinates targeting an empty nearby hill. I sat down with the platoon sergeant and started chatting while we opened some god awful "C" rations. A battery of high explosive rounds came pouring in. We never even looked up. A perimeter artillery strike was part of the everyday routine. Immediately after the rounds exploded however, an odd high pitched whistling noise started. We were always listening for unusual noises which could be our only warning of enemy activity. The platoon sergeant and I looked at each other. This was trouble. We were sitting down; there was no time to move. The whistling got louder. A few seconds later a spinning piece of shrapnel slammed into the ground eighteen inches to my right. Had I dove to my right for cover, that would have been it. The shrapnel was the same size as a kitchen knife blade and smoking hot. The platoon sergeant grabbed a towel from his backpack, pulled the shrapnel out of the ground, and went to have a few words with our new Forward Observer.

Sergeant "Little Jack's" nerves were about gone. He kept waking up at night screaming. He could no longer sleep with a revolver under his belt for fear he would kill one of us by accident. Someone told me Little Jack had seen some awful things. His problem got worse until finally I radioed the rear and had some "Librium" sent out to him. I kept the medicine for him at his own request.

About a day after the delivery of Librium, Little Jack left for a rear job. He never asked me for his medicine and I forgot to give it to him. So I kept the Librium and occasionally passed it out to the men. They never said they were nervous, just that they "couldn't sleep".

Artillery shells were always falling around us. I was far more afraid of our artillery than I was the enemy. One night I lay in my hammock and listened to heavy metal canisters crashing through tree limbs around us. They were falling from spent illumination rounds. I didn't think that the fire base targeted the canisters as carefully as they did the artillery rounds. I lay in my hammock, wished the night was over, and threw a Librium into the back of my mouth.

"Doc have you ever seen a dead dink?" Big Jim Butler's words rolled with his Alabama drawl. Big Jim was sort of a folk hero in the company. There was something genuinely heroic about him. Everybody liked and respected him. Only a few nights before we had heard his voice shouting above his blazing pig, "I'll keep their gawd damned heads down." He did just that. Now his voice called to me.

"No", I answered. Jim said "Well then, come here".

I moved forward from my position behind the surrounding grass. I hadn't moved too close to Jim before because the stench was so bad. We had killed two N.V.A. three days before. I remember hearing "There's the son of a bitch." (High pitched) "Kill him! Kill him!" The two soldiers had hit one of our mines and dragged themselves into the bush. We heard groaning amid their wild desperate fire. Our boys tracked them down and finished them off.

Now the killing was over for a moment and we were preparing for more. We had come back as a squad to attach mines to the bodies so that if their comrades came back to claim them, they too would be shredded.

The dead soldier I was staring at was an N.V.A. regular, tough looking with a military hair cut, and handsome. I think he was missing an arm. Somebody in our company was enjoying a three day pass for having set the mine. Pan Am had brought us to Vietnam from Seattle. This man had walked from Hanoi. I wondered if he had left a family. Our men set out the booby traps and we left.

Another ambush. Whenever we stayed in any one place for any one time, somebody would be sent out to set up an ambush. So we sat as comfortably as we could in the jungle foliage. We were in a shallow ravine. At the bottom of the ravine lay a small, cool stream, an oasis on a long hike. Across from us on the other side of the ravine, a seldom used N.V.A. trail wound down to the stream.

The minutes dragged on. In a few more weeks the bananas hanging above us might be edible. At the moment they didn't even look appetizing to us, despite the fact that we had been on "C" rations for months. That gives you an idea how bad those bananas looked.

Suddenly a barrage of artillery shells landed on the ridge lying opposite our position. It was close, but we didn't think too much of it. The artillery was often close.

Nothing happened during the ambush, but I learned later on that the purpose of the artillery fire was to drive any enemy soldiers that might have been on the ridge opposite us, into us. Our position in the ravine had not been good. Had enemy soldiers come down that trail, the only thing between us and their bullets would have been the leaves of plants. I suppose the artillery fire was a wise tactical move dreamed up by somebody with a pencil and a map. But after that incident I was bitter. I felt I had been used.

We were set in for the night. Joe had taken his squad out to watch over a mechanical ambush. I set up my hammock and then noticed that I was sleeping over an old unexploded 105 round. It looked rusty, so I figured it probably wouldn't go off during the night. We were to the point where we were used to living with explosives.

Joe's Claymore booby trap exploded. Silence. Then the sound of M16's firing in the distance. Joe's M-70 popped a grenade. Mike (our Lieutenant) jumped up and down, "We got one! We got a dink!" The hunt was on; the madness was complete. More fire. The whole squad opened up.

There was trouble. We hadn't got the dink after all. Instead, Joe and his men were being hunted. In the dusk, someone had crept up to the booby trap, disconnected the wires to the Claymore's battery, undone the trip wire, picked the mine up, turned it around until it pointed to where he thought Joe's squad was sitting in ambush, reconnected the battery, ran his own trip wire back to a safe distance and jerked it. What guts. Fortunately there was a ninety degree bend in the trail between the mine and Joe's men. The mine blew right past them. Those mines are incredibly deadly. If the trail had been straight... I don't even want to think about it. Realizing that cover had been blown (literally), Joe's men opened up with everything they had and sprayed the area. In the evening shadows, they hit nothing.

The following was written by a Vietnamese Buddhist monk:

Men kill because on the one hand they do not know their real enemy, and on the other hand, they have been pushed into a position where they cannot not kill.

Let me tell you what happened to Duc last year. He was waiting for a civilian plane at a small isolated airport in the highlands, along with five or six young American soldiers who were waiting for a Karibou plane to fly them on a search and destroy operation. There was no one else besides them. One of the young soldiers struck up a conversation with Duc, who immediately saw that the American knew absolutely nothing about Vietnamese history and culture or the truth of the conflict in which he was playing a part. He was certain of only one thing; the V.C. was his enemy. His duty was, as he put it, to destroy the V.C. in order to save the Vietnamese and the free world. Duc was very, very sad. He asked the G.I., "Do you fear the V.C.?" At that question the soldier leapt abruptly to his feet. Duc saw that his eyes were alarmed and suspicious; suspicious that the questioner might be a V.C. He had been told again and again that the V.C were a very cunning bunch and since he was afraid of them, wherever he went, at whatever time, he imagined that the V.C. were present. So he asked rapidly, on his guard, "Are you a V.C.?" Duc thought that the question was very funny but he did not dare smile. He saw fear, real fear in the soldier's eyes. He knew that, if, in a joking spirit he said "Yes", the soldier would shoot him. So he answered "No" and explained that he was a Professor and was only waiting to catch a plane back to Saigon. You know what Duc said after he had told us about his "adventure"? He said that if he had been killed then, it would not have been because the American soldier wanted to kill him. The soldier only wanted to kill Vietcong. He could hate the V.C. only because he really did not know what the V.C. were. He imagined that they were monsters – wild, cruel monsters that had to be hunted down. In his country the people are fed so much of this that they keep on letting their government send men over here to kill and

66

be killed. So, men kill unjustly and in turn are killed unjustly...... and it is precisely their own compatriots who kill them. They are the ones who are really responsible for the massacre of our people but they go on deluding themselves that they do not have anything actually to do with it because they do not hold a gun and pull the trigger. Who really kills them? Their own fear, hatred, ignorance, and prejudice.

Author's name unknown.

We had just killed a woman. She was carrying rice to an N.V.A. outpost. She was running in the distance and we couldn't tell that she was a woman. I wonder if it would have made any difference if we had known. For the first time as I am writing this, I'm beginning to feel that we were villains stifling a basically heroic effort by the Vietnamese.

Dean pinned her down with machine gun fire then Mike, my close friend, called the artillery in on top of her. Twenty minutes later we had cut our way through the jungle to where we thought she was. We constructed a night position while a squad looked for our victim. Finally they found her; she had crawled off a way from the trail. I found out later that her shoulder and cheek had been blown off by one of the artillery shells. She died in the medivac chopper.

When the squad returned, I overheard that our "kill" was female. "A woman!" I explained. Captain Harley said "Doc, she played the game and she lost." A cliché. Two weeks later, Captain Harley was dead. That was a real nightmare. He was all Army, but courageous and took chances with his own life to capture prisoners of war instead of killing them. He was a big, strong man, aggressive and responsible. But in social situations he was shy and quiet like a young boy. I liked him.

On the first re-supply chopper after Captain Harley's death, Mike, the Lieutenant whose platoon I had spent a lot of time with, came out with the supplies. He was saying goodbye to us before his return to the States. They brought Captain Harley's bullet riddled gear to the chopper. I turned to Mike and said "I couldn't believe it when I heard he had died in surgery. The news came over our radio the day before. There is no silence in the world as deep as the silence that fell over us when we heard he was dead. Mike replied "That's war, Doc." Another cliché. What the cliché says is true. But it's still a cliché and a poor substitute for human feeling. I could not then, nor will I ever be able to accept clichés in return for human life.

Firebase Raw Hide

Lots of artillery, dust and germs. Concertina wire between us and a placid village scene, creating an illusion of safety. A barracks with holes ripped through its metal roof tells of raining mortar shells and screaming nights. But for weeks now the only sounds had come from our own artillery. Christmas lights turning from green into red walking footprints of death across an evening landscape. Now the quiet afternoon. My daily labors had settled along with the dust kicked up by the helicopters taking off and landings. Everyone had their appropriate medication.

"Doc!" Smitty left his beer and radio. Smitty was a good man slowly becoming more anti-war from being with his fellow soldiers. "Doc!" they're flying in a wounded civilian." OK. Get it together. Grab the right bag. I was respected for my work in Vietnam. They always came to me when something was seriously wrong. Strut! Pride! Responsibility… the first in my life. I served them well. I acted out my role with gusto. I belonged.

"Doc, she's a woman." Bits of information tumbled out of Smitty's radio. "Badly burned." Grab another bandage bag. Might need a stretcher.

I began the quarter mile jog to the helicopter pad with heavy bags and a stretcher. Don Quixote tilting towards a whirlybird windmill. Another medic was already there. He turned from the helicopter with a "do something" look on his face. With bursting legs I finally arrived at the helicopter door. The patient was a baby. Helicopter blades drowning out all other sounds; all other concerns. A baby. Her tiny hand and foot barely hung on by threads of torn flesh. She wasn't breathing. I touched her head and turned it from side to side. Still supple and warm; must have just stopped breathing. No bleeding. For a few seconds I stood frozen. Someone grabbed the child by the towel she was laying on and carried her to a waiting transport chopper that would take her to a medivac station. I followed. The child, too fragile to survive in this world, lay between the door gunner's feet. All conversation is with hand gestures. "Shouldn't I carry her in my arms so she won't fall out?" Solemnly shaking my head, "Just go!" Translation; "get this unacceptable horror out of my sight."

Later justifications for having not breathed for the child:

She was already dead.

What chance would a child without a hand and foot and parents have had in that war torn Vietnamese culture?

The truth is obvious.

Later our battalion commander gathered us around to see if anyone felt a war crime had been committed. It was true that no one knew that three women and two babies were in that bunker. Our troops had received enemy fire from that area, and heard voices in the bunker and had thrown in a hand grenade. One soldier in our group yelled out "We've got to forget it! That's all, just forget it!" Later I thought; How can we pour all this fire power into a third world country and have the audacity to be surprised when this kind of thing happens?

As it turned out it was one of the soldier's birthday. Someone had somehow constructed a birthday cake. So I invited the Colonel to join us for a brief celebration. I liked him. He was a good man. It was just another day.

England, June 23rd, 2008

I was proud of the soldiers I served with in Vietnam. The vast majority of them were good solid souls, brave and full of life. They were the best of what the United States had to offer. But as stated before, we were all victims of historical circumstance. When my comrades in arms were in junior high school, they didn't expect to be living one day at a time in the jungles of Vietnam. They were also betrayed by a United States government that didn't do its homework. Not only did our policy makers fail to historically understand what was going on in Vietnam, there was also an arrogance, at least initially, that our bombs would deal with all the problems. Our soldiers were also betrayed by a public that reviled them when they returned home after risking their lives for a year.

The North Vietnamese army soldiers were no group of angels. You did not want to be captured by them, nor did you want to be a Vietnamese civilian found aiding the U.S military effort. The North Vietnamese soldiers were ruthless, brave, efficient and victorious. That's about all you can say.

What you didn't hear a lot about were the millions of Vietnamese civilians caught in the middle of the war. All they wanted to do was plant their rice fields and raise their kids. But if you add the two Indo Chinese wars to the Vietnam conflict, all these people had was one decade of bloody war after another. There are hundreds of thousands of stories involving suffering and hardship that will never be told. Who stands behind these nameless people? Who protects and comforts them?

About a decade ago, I sat next to a professor of Political Science on a flight from London to Boston. I would gladly give him credit for the following story, but I lost his business card and have no way of contacting him.

The thrust of what his academic department tried to do was to bring resolution to major world conflicts. Toward that end, they arranged for Robert McNamara to pay a visit to North Vietnam after the war and visit with the political powers that be. Robert McNamara, the former Secretary of State under Kennedy and Johnson, had just written a book detailing how the American public had been deliberately misled about the events surrounding the Vietnam war. It took a lot of courage to write that book, although it would have been better to publish that information during the actual conflict. But, better late than never.

Soon after arriving in Vietnam, McNamara, my professor friend and a few others were having breakfast in a Hanoi hotel. The waitress serving them stopped and stared for a moment. She then asked "Are you Robert McNamara?" Oh oh! A very large cat was out of the bag. One of the major architects of the Vietnam war was having breakfast in her hotel. She rapidly disappeared back into the kitchen. The American party started looking around for emergency exits. Suddenly the doors to the kitchen flew open. Instead of kitchen knives, the hotel staff were waving copies of McNamara's book. It had been translated into Vietnamese and was the number one best seller in Vietnam. They all lined up so McNamara could sign their copies of the book. Whew!

The Vietnamese will never forget what happened to them in the Vietnam War, nor should they. I am told there is a very powerful museum in Hanoi that documents the War's events. But, unlike many cultures in similar situations, the Vietnamese have found the strength to move on. In fact, shortly after the fall of Saigon, it was the Vietnamese army that stopped the Cambodian Communist monster Pol Pot in his tracks. Without that intervention, Pol Pot's grotesque slaughter of Cambodian civilians would have continued unabated. What irony. So much for the domino theory.

Chapter IV

LEMMINGS TO THE SEA

Humanity's unrelenting need to follow a leader seems to be a stronger drive than the need to question the quality of that leadership. In other words, we line up to do the bidding of some very questionable people.

But before we launch into the serious issues, let's look at the lighter side of that problem. In no other arena does humanity's blind need to follow the herd express itself with such comic potential as it does in the fashion industry. In essence, the fashion industry is the rich and powerful telling the weak minded how to look. Billions of dollars are spent every year creating and marketing the latest well advertised fashion trend. God forbid you would be out of step with the absurd looking outpatients from the bulimia clinic that parade across the pages of the fashion magazines. Eating disorders are a common and very serious problem among teenage girls. The fashion industry knows this, but continues to advertise waif like images that encourage young girls to engage in this potentially lethal behavior.

As far as I can tell, the point of the whole mammoth fashion exercise is to get yourself noticed. For what it's worth, if your smile and the warmth of your personality doesn't attract him, the two thousand dollar fashion accessory certainly won't help your cause. Having lots of Gucci will not prevent you from ending up alone.

All of this has to do with our need to feel special, and at the same time accepted by society. The fashion industry is perceived as moving us toward those goals because their products are so highly visible. It only takes a moment to look at someone, and in that moment we must be seen as desirable. Learning how to relate to others in a genuine and positive manner takes a lot more work.

73

But the fashion industry is only one superficial example of how meeting our needs can be perverted and twisted into something very sinister. The bottom line is that our fundamental desires can be used by truly evil people in a way that will result in unbelievably destructive behavior. That destructive behavior is a manifestation of the psychopathology of the leader who is doing the manipulating. It's all done with smoke and mirrors, feeds on people's fears and vulnerabilities, and eventually results in a grotesque catalogue of carnage that historians end up recording years later. This downhill cascade of events often begins with just one sociopathic individual.

Most sociopaths exhibit a highly self-destructive tendency which often limits their potential for causing pain to others. Many of them wind up on drugs or alcohol, steal, maybe kill a few people, sperm donor a small group of totally whacked out kids, abuse spouses and drive the local social services crazy. Only the truly stupid or like minded would follow these folk. Their overall damage to society is usually muted by the local police. But once in a while a sociopath comes along who is both extremely intelligent and charismatic. Take that sociopath's ability to persuade the masses, add to it some serious nationwide economic instability, and you have the recipe for true and complete disaster. The millions and millions of innocent people who perished violently in the twentieth century died as a result of the policies of only a handful of sociopathic maniacs. Hitler, Stalin, Pol Pot, Idi Amin, Sadam Hussein, and whoever orchestrated the Rwanda massacre are obviously some of the major players. But the key point is that these monsters cannot physically kill millions of people themselves. Instead they create an infrastructure of tens of thousands of weak minded and ignorant people who carry out their leader's atrocities. What is truly sickening is that time and again people line up to do the monster's bidding. They just can't wait to serve, to be part of the larger group.

Invariably there is an ideology concocted to make these obscene acts palatable to the general public. You would think that the defects inherent in that ideology (i.e. the Master Race) would be obvious, but the frenzy of the mob just seems to erase common sense. Everyone wants to join what everyone else is doing, no matter how blatantly insane the results of those actions might be. It is also probably a survival instinct in going with, instead of against, the social tide.

One milestone of morality, and I would argue, a major key to a happy and fulfilling life is a person's ability to think independently. I'm not talking about the obnoxious and immature habit of giving the finger to all forms of authority. Instead, I'm talking about the ability to honestly and objectively evaluate any given situation based on its own merits. What's needed to perform that type of evaluation is a dedication to the idea that what is true matters more than God, Country or anything else. In order for that objectivity to exist, one's sense of self value has to transcend what the rest of the herd thinks of you. That doesn't mean that you ignore other people's opinions or reject all advice. Sometimes other people can see things more clearly than we do. But, in essence, someone at some point has to be willing to speak the truth and be willing to take the consequences of that action.

One important lesson that came out of the invasion of Iraq is that if a true psychopathic despot has been in charge of a country for decades, then that country cannot be put right in a short amount of time. That's because even though you cut off the head of the snake by taking out the chief monster, the little monsters that carried out the big monster's orders still exist. A whole infrastructure survives that is corrupt, evil and without compassion. The little monsters also want to return to the special status they had when the chief monster was in charge. Throughout the decades of governmental power being abused most of the good folk were either killed or fled. Everyone else who couldn't flee either cooperated with the despot or kept their heads down and simply hoped for the best. I have to laugh at the idea that a monster has sovereignty over his own country. If the monster's people are being systematically raped, tortured and murdered, how can that monster's government claim the right to sovereignty? Is mass murder acceptable as long as one keeps it in their own back yard?

Years ago while doing a student rotation in the United States, I worked with a fellow who was visiting from Iraq. In an effort to make conversation over lunch I asked him what it was like to live in Iraq. He stayed silent. After a few weeks, I was no longer a stranger to him. Only then did he answer my question. He said "My country is a terrible place! It is run by a butcher. Sadam goes out and practices killing people by executing condemned prisoners himself. In my country many people go around asking the same question you asked me at lunch weeks ago. If I give the wrong answer, I disappear". He was a good man. He kept his head down.

The Nazis of the Third Reich did not evolve in some third world back water. They came to power in one of the most scientifically and culturally sophisticated countries in the world. This means that no culture is immune to homicidal mass psychosis. The sign in front of Dachau says "Never again"; but it did happen again, in Srebrenitza, North Korea, South East Asia, Rwanda and Darfur. Rwandan Hutus went out and hacked to death villagers they had been living next to for decades. The only reason given for this atrocity was that the authorities told them to do it. The insanity of that seems so blatant. One can only conclude that as a species we have a very flat learning curve.

One key to understanding how these senseless slaughters can occur again and again is to simply understand how endemic evil is within humanity. There is no escaping that harsh reality. We all want world peace. We all sing the songs extolling the "Brotherhood of Man". But the bad news is that world peace is never going to happen. That doesn't mean that we don't go out and try to make the world a better place. What it does mean is that the next great monster is a kid somewhere, torturing small animals and making his classmates nervous. The only thing that will enable that monster to come to power is the people who will fall in line behind him. The herd will unrelentingly carry him to a place where he can carry out his homicidal ideology.

There is no limit to people's ability to delude themselves. The psycho who created an army of drugged children in Africa ordered, among other things, that all white chickens should be killed. Well, why not follow a guy like that? Everyone knows how demonic white chickens are.

It's only a matter of time before we see another Jones Town cool aid happy hour, or worse, much worse. People desperately need to be told their place within society, and some sociopathic lunatic will always be more than happy to do just that.

Chapter V

DEGREE No.3

As I walked into the P.A. program's classroom, I once again found myself mingling with a very diverse group of people. There was a group of ex Army medics, mostly composed of minorities. They had just signed a very promising contract with the city of New York. In return for three year's work in New York City clinics after graduation, the city would pay for the student's entire education. That's a good deal. But there was a problem. They were up against the other half of the class, which I can only describe as academic whiz kids. They all had their undergraduate degree, but for whatever reason had failed to get into medical school. The wiz kids were high powered and intelligent. They believed that becoming a Physician's Assistant would help their future efforts to get into medical school. That turned out to be a smart move. Most of them went on to become physicians.

But the wiz kids knew all the ins and outs of the academic game. They were professional test takers. There was no way the inner city minorities could compete with them. One by one most of the minority students fell by the wayside. One of them said to me "All my life I've taken a lot of pride in viewing myself as a reasonably intelligent man, and these *kids* are making me look like an *idiot!*" The school was vitally interested in establishing itself as having a program with solid credentials. The only way to document that was with good test scores. As the minority students left the program, I felt that a lot of real potential was going down the drain.

As time went on, the surviving students formed study groups. We spent our evenings firing endless amounts of questions back and forth. Friendships developed. We were trying to absorb a whole new world. Tests came and went. After the first academic year I had six weeks off. I ran (actually flew) back to the High Sierra mountains. My brain desperately needed some clean, fresh unoxygenated air. It worked. A purely physical experience and endless vistas worked their restorative magic.

The program's first year did have one high point. They brought in a Pakistani physician from a Brooklyn hospital to teach us cardiology. He was both intimidating and brilliant. After years of playing the academic game you quickly learn when you have stumbled upon a really good teacher. In academics you don't take courses, you take professors. A bad teacher can make a course on "The Grand Unification Theory" a sleep inducing experience. On the other hand, a good professor can teach a course on basket weaving techniques and make your eyes open in amazement. This cardiologist was a top notch instructor. He lectured us for months. If you missed one lecture, you were lost. He never used notes; it was all in his head. What he was doing was providing a firm foundation for our understanding of the physiology and pathology of the human heart. The cardiology training I later received in medical school could not come close to what I received in my Physicians Assistant program.

I thought "I can't let this go to waste.", so I did what any good student would do. I found an excellent Chinese Restaurant. After all nothing good happens without oral rewards. The small Brooklyn Chinese hole in the wall restaurant had fourteen options for dinner. I would order one of those fourteen choices and open up the day's cardiology notes. Everything was fresh in my mind because our cardiology lectures usually occurred at the end of the day. I then developed a neat little academic trick. I would take what I thought was an important piece of information from the notes and turn that information into a question. For example, I would write on the left side of a piece of paper "What are the physical signs of congestive heart failure?" On the right side of the paper I would list the answers to that question. This technique accomplishes several goals. First, if you can form the information into a question, then you understand that information. Then when test time comes around, you have a notebook (or three) full of test questions. Just cover the answers and ask yourself the questions. If you don't know the answers all you have to do is uncover the right half of the page. Then after you've gone through the questions once, go through it all again trying to answer the questions that you missed the first time around. If you think a certain question is really a key point in the lecture put a star beside it. Make sure you have the star questions down cold before you go into a test. This system really works. Studies have shown that if you just write down what the professor says, the information is lost with the first good party. You might retain 15% of the lecture content on a good day. But I found that my question and answer technique raised long term information retention to about 60%.

There are two disadvantages to this method of study:

1. It's time consuming. A lot of Chinese food went down.
2. You have to choose which information to put into a question. Invariably, you will leave some important information out.

Therefore this technique is not the best for scoring 95 to 100% on an exam. But on the other hand, using this study technique makes it really difficult to fail an exam.

But this question and answer process does something much more important than just allowing you to pass exams. It develops understanding. As stated before, you have to work the information through your mind. I had old notes from college where the ink mark half way through a sentence would slide down the page accompanied by dried up drool from my semi comatose mouth. The professor was reading his lecture in a non-stop and monotone manner. Just give me the sleeping pill when I come into the classroom and the same result will occur with much less effort.

But as I sat with my crispy fried duck, I knew something very different was happening. As luck would have it, my medical residency was done in a cardiac referral center. Day after day I put my cardiology knowledge to use. When it came time for me to work as a medical attending in an emergency room, cardiology became my ace in the deck. I wasn't afraid of it (outside of the fact that the patient could die at any moment). Our little hospital was tied for the second best cardiac survival rate in the state. Part of the reason for that rating was that one man, Dr Mohammed Zahir, really knew how to teach.

Chapter VI

DIRECT SALES

In the late 1970s I decided to take a new direction in terms of vocation. I answered a friendly looking ad in the newspaper and became a salesman. My product was double glazed doors and windows. Well, after all, why not? My Dad was a huge success in sales. His honesty and dedication to the customer set a high standard. Once people found out that his word was as good as gold, customers beat a path to his door. In his first two years in direct sales he sold one fourth of the company's entire product. He was simply a natural with people. He eventually became the company's C.E.O. He also invented one of their largest selling products. Not bad for having started out in a coal mine. He truly lived the American dream. Why couldn't I do the same thing? So, as naive as a human being can be, I walked into direct sales. ("Direct" means you deal face to face with the customer).

As a result of my work selling doors and windows I learned a few things. First of all, believe it or not, you can over insulate a house. No one would argue that insulating a house to save on fuel bills isn't a smart idea, but you have to know what you are doing. A house, like a human being, has to be able to breathe. Human beings produce a surprising amount of moisture during exhalation. That moisture has to have a way of exiting the house. In the summertime it's not an issue because the windows are open. But in the winter an air tight house will trap moisture. If you see water droplets day after day on the inside of your windows, you will eventually end up with some serious wood rot.

Basically a house can be insulated in three ways:

1. Replacing the doors and windows with a product that is double glazed

2. Pouring insulation into the walls
3. Insulating the roof

As a general rule, it's best to do two out of three of those options thus leaving moisture a necessary exit. In other words don't insulate the house to the point where everything is nailed completely shut.

The second thing I learned is that people who have made a lifelong career doing direct sales know more about applied human psychology than anyone with a PhD in that subject. The salesman's living depends on his ability to get people to do what he wants them to do. The relevancy of that skill will become clear in a minute.

Modern insulated windows are really a remarkable creation. The glass is of such high quality that you can have two or three panes of glass (double or triple glazing) between you and what you are looking at outside and the image you see will not be distorted. The frame is enameled aluminum which is light and strong. There are multiple tracks in which the panes of glass sit. The windows will not only slide up and down, but on turning a few plastic levers, will open inwards so that you can clean the entire window from the inside of the house. Where moving parts touch they are lined with a wool like fuzzy substance that further seals the window. There are no open cracks to the outside and the windows need almost no maintenance. There's just one little problem. A product of this quality is really expensive. Not only does it cost a lot to make, but the sales have to cover everyone's pay check in the company plus a profit. When you tell potential customers that replacing their doors and windows will cost as much as it did for them to buy their entire house twenty five years ago, you might as well just pack up your sales gear and leave. When they hear how much the job will cost there is usually an audible gasp.

But the salesman has an answer to this problem. Let's say the entire job plus your commission costs $18,500. Instead of saying "Guess what folks, the doors and windows along with installation will cost $18,500!", the salesman instead does the unthinkable. He blows the customers right out of the water. He tells them that the job will cost $34,000. After they recover from that piece of information with the help of intravenous sedating drugs, the salesman then goes to work. It's important that the customers know that the salesman wants them to have this great product.

The salesman has just spent an hour demonstrating portable window samples followed by a display of photographs showing actual finished jobs. That demonstration conclusively proved the value of these products. Furthermore the salesman has placed in front of them charts and graphs that demonstrate how in a few decades the insulated doors and windows will actually save enough on fuel bills to pay for the entire installation. Obviously the salesman is on their side. He wants to help them.

After the demonstration the salesman expresses his understanding that $34,000 is completely out of their reach (remember this is the 1970s). But fortunately for the customers the company is currently running a series of specials to expand their market in this time of rapidly rising fuel prices. If the customers will permit a series of before and after photographs to be taken of their house (someone will actually come out with a camera) and then allow those photographs to be used in a double glazing advertising blitz, the company will reduce the purchase price by $3,000. O.K, that's all well and good, but their car has been giving them some difficulties and they just cannot part with $31,000 right now. But wait, there's more. If they are willing to have the company's logo placed on a sign in their front yard for ninety days after the installation, that will reduce the price by another $2,500. Sometimes neighbors will admire the work and want the replacement windows for themselves, and that's good for the company. Now we are down to $28,500. The barrier of $30,000 is a thing of the past. But it gets even better. More specials follow until the price falls to around $24,500, but that's the bottom line. After all the company has saved them almost $10,000. What more could they ask for?

The salesman then sits with the customers and chats over a cup of coffee for about another twenty minutes. He lets them talk about the cold draft that comes in at night through the cracks in their current windows. They know that their home heating system is warming the entire neighborhood. The fiberglass they put in the attic helped, but just wasn't enough.

At this point the salesman starts to open his mouth, but then hesitates. They become curious. The salesman says, "I really shouldn't bring this up. Our company was having a huge promotion, but it just ended two days ago". Their shoulders fall. What was this missed opportunity? Their curiosity grows. The salesman leans back and says, "Well the high quality glass in our windows is made by a company that also makes windshields for a major car company" (This is actually true. The glass company's name is on the windows). "The glass company is trying to broaden their customer base in the replacement window market. Part of their promotional effort consisted of dividing our state in to five districts. They then poured about two million dollars into the state. Each district received a portion of that two million. The parcels of money were called allotments. Any customer who purchased the windows last month got a slice of those allotments. Some of the savings were really substantial. But unfortunately I know that all the money allocated to region five has already been given out to customers. Your house is located in region five. It's too bad". More silence. Then the salesman puts down his coffee cup and says "I could get into real trouble for this, but I know that there is still some allotment money left in region three. Sales last month in that region were disappointing. I could call my sales manager and see if he would be willing to move some of that remaining money from region three into region five. However we're really not supposed to do this. In fact, the last time I tried it, I woke the sales manager up and he got really angry. I had better not do it". Invariably the customers will ask ,"Well, how much would that allotment money amount to in our case?" So the salesman gets out his calculator, takes a few minutes, and announces that the allotment money would reduce the price of their purchase to $18,500. That's amazing! Now you have the customer's full attention. After all $18,500 is a drop in the bucket when compared to $34,000. They know they need this great product. They are being offered an unbelievable savings of forty six percent. So the salesman says, "Look, if I take a chance on waking up my boss (it's now 10.00 pm) and manage to get you this enormous savings, will you buy the product?" In sales this question is called "the commitment". If the salesman is willing to go way out of his way to help you out, you have to be willing to complete the deal. If the customer says "Yes" and makes the salesman do significant work and then backs out of the deal, the customer looks like a complete jerk. So now the customer has an emotional stake in completing the purchase.

The salesman asks if he can use the customer's phone. He dials a number and waits a few seconds before speaking. Uh oh, he did wake the sales manager up at home. The sales manager is not pleased. But the salesman argues with him that these customers are nice people and really need the product. He describes their current pathetic windows and pleads "Can't we cut them a break?"

Now any customer with brains might begin to smell a rat. All of this is simply too good to be true. So the wife might sneak into the bedroom and pick up the extension phone to see if the salesman is actually talking to someone. Low and behold, she will hear the salesman conversing with an irritated gentleman. That gentleman is paid to wait by his phone at night. He is extensively trained on how to argue with the salesman. Amazingly enough after about five minutes, the salesman wins the argument. The money is shifted from region three to region five and, against all odds, the immense savings are obtained. The deal is finalized.

But the salesman cannot leave the house just yet. Instead he continues to chat for about another twenty to thirty minutes. He does this because customer concerns will arise. When will the job be done? Will the house be freezing cold while the work is being completed? One by one, the salesman puts all of these concerns to rest. This is called "closing the sale". Afterwards, holding a down payment check and a signed contract, the salesman calls it a night.

We did provide a good product at a fair price, but the whole manipulation song and dance bothered me. I was even using some of my psychotherapy techniques to complete my sales. So one day I said to myself "I'm a straightforward guy with a good product. I can sell these windows without playing any games". So I tried it. I went into people's homes and truthfully and clearly presented all the product's qualities and advantages. I fell flat on my face every time. As soon as the customers heard the real price for our service, their wallets and ass holes slammed shut at exactly the same time.

People still function on a level of basic survival instincts. For example if a primitive tribe is starving and stumbles on a previously undiscovered grove of fruit trees, you want to be one of those tribal members taking advantage of that discovery. You don't want to be cleaning out the huts at home while everyone else is stuffing their faces. Instead, you want to be doing the face stuffing. Let some other poor slob clean out the huts. We all want to be in on the action. The salesman creates that opportunity, whether real or imagined.

Over time I began to realize that the company was using me the same way we used the customers. There were no benefits with the job. There was no car allowance, even though we might drive several hundred miles a week going to people's home. In fact, we didn't get paid a dime until after the customers completed their payment. On a bad sales month, you might barely make food money. In addition, the chalk board in the sales room (which was hidden from public view) listed the month's individual sales as "Kills". It was time for me to go.

As a footnote, in our consumer driven culture it is worthwhile to realize that we are being sold something almost constantly. The advertisements are everywhere. Our kids are watching them. The first thing a company does is to create a need. For example, they might convince the majority of women that they must have wrinkle free skin. Well, why not have a face that is ageless and at the same time completely devoid of character? Every day companies are competing to answer your needs whether those needs are real or imagined. How lucky can you get? After all, you're worth it.

Chapter VII

ON RELIGION Part A

Cyprus
May 2007

Y ou may have heard of a group called "Jews for Jesus." There is even a group called "Truckers for Jesus." But when I was in college, I was without question a "Robot for Jesus." Looking back on the writings I did at that time, they are a source of true embarrassment. How could anyone have listened to me? I had no soul. I wasn't really grounded in anything. I was nothing more than a string of religious clichés. I had all the answers as laid out in the Bible. There was right and wrong, saved and unsaved, black and white, God's truth and man's sin. There was never any shade of grey in my thinking. I was inflexible, inexperienced and pathetic. The truth is that in those early years I actually hated myself, but at the time I wasn't even aware of that.

But it gets worse. About the only way I could relate to people was through their problems. Without a soul of my own, what else could I do? So if people didn't have problems, I found it difficult to connect to them. What a sick existence.

The only thing that saved me in the long run was that in everything I did, I was absolutely sincere. Therefore when I saw flaws in my faith's unwavering interpretation of reality, I couldn't turn my back on those inconsistencies. For example, there were a number of unsaved students on campus who really enjoyed their lives. I wanted them to be my friends. Emotionally I could trust them. On the other hand, the born again folk really sent a shiver up my spine. For most of them their psychiatric illnesses were obvious. They were a collection of religious clichés forming a dome over a cauldron of unmet needs and inflexible personalities. In other words, they were just like me. The idea of being saved and spending eternity with these folk filled me with horror.

After years in the born again realm I grew intolerant of what I will call "reflexive thinking." By "reflexive thinking" I mean religious people giving you the answers to life's problems when you know they never even heard the questions in the first place. Problem "A" is automatically met with religious cliché "B". More robots, more pamphlets. Some part of me knew that I could never grow in that rigid religious environment. As previously stated, the day after I graduated from college I threw a sleeping bag into the trunk of my car and headed for the national parks of the great south west. It was time to embark on a journey of my own. Fresh air and fresh thinking were desperately needed. I had an intense hunger for something real and concrete. The endless highways and vistas that stretched before me were exhilarating and full of possibilities. That trip led me to take an irreversible step. I left the Church.

All of the above experiences now make it difficult for me to write about religion. Thirty years after exiting the Church, it's still hard for me to see the religious forest for the unending doctrinal trees. Religion is a highly emotional issue, which makes true objectivity a real challenge. After years of thinking about religion for this book, I knew that my approach to this complicated subject had to be kept very simple. Lots of philosophical details would only act as a confusing distraction. Therefore no detailed lengthy religious treatise will follow. If I can hopefully make a few simple and pragmatic points, so much the better. So fasten your theological seat belts. Here we go.

The primary question facing religion in today's world centers around the body count. How many millions of innocent people have been tortured and murdered over the ages for no other reason than the fact that they did not belong to the dominant religion or sect of their time? How many men, women and children have screamed in pain and fear? Only the great natural disasters (plagues, earthquakes etc.) or major wars of conquest can claim more total bloodshed than religion. What an agonizing travesty. What a collection of human failings and all in the name of God.

The history of religion is so full of violence that a rational argument can be made that humanity would be better off if religion did not exist.

But religion is never going to vanish because humanity is religious by nature. Even the most primitive cultures have elaborate creation myths and rituals. Perhaps we just cannot stand the idea that we are spinning through the blackness of space completely vulnerable to disease and natural disasters. Our collective response to the scary idea that we are totally helpless and alone is to invent some sort of religious touchstone. We need a God.

But regardless of the motivations for religious beliefs, the problem of religious mayhem finds its roots in human nature. As a species we are violent, competitive and tribal. We had to be all of those things through the ages in order to survive. If you were non violent and without a tribe in Neolithic times, you died. In those days there was a distinct absence of social services. Let's face it, the guy with the biggest stick managed to thrive, have lots of sex and make the rules. Christ was murdered because he tried to change human nature (love your enemies etc.) and people simply couldn't do it. He also spit in the face of the religious hierarchy of his day, and that is never consistent with longevity. So, over the millennium man keeps creating God in his own image which is violent, tribal and competitive. Let's take this concept down to a simple example. If you have two societies living on two large islands that are separated by, say fifty miles of water, in all probability those two societies will eventually go to war. The reasons for the war may vary, but the result will be the same. The vanquished men will be killed, the women raped and the children made into slaves. That's how it goes. That's what we do.

A similar chain of events will occur between another two groups; the saved and the unsaved. Once you separate human beings into those who are the sheep and those who are the goats, it's only a matter of time before the sheep take out the goats. After all, the faith must be purified. The stain and contamination of the unbelievers has to be removed. Only then can God be worshipped in the "right" way. This literal way of thinking has repeatedly resulted in all holy hell being unleashed on earth.

You may have noted that religious violence is particularly heinous. That's because no matter what awful act the religious followers commit, God will make it all better in the afterlife. Therefore compassion is a waste of time. For instance, after a suicide bomber blows up a bus, he must stand in front of Allah and ask each child that has been shredded by shrapnel for forgiveness. Well that's all right then! Bombs away! No matter how horrendous the act, the slate will eventually be wiped clean because it's all Gods' will. How very convenient.

Getting back to the basics of human nature, as human competitiveness descends deeper into evil, greed and the lust for power become more evident. At this point I digress to my childhood. During my upbringing I received a total of about five lines of advice from my father. He came home one evening after a grueling day in the corporate world, sat in his overstuffed chair, looked down at the floor, shook his grey head, picked up his pipe and glanced over at me. He said "Sam, the greatest human failing is greed." He did not elaborate. He just lit his pipe, sat back in his chair and stared into the distance with his soft blue eyes. It took me until my adult years to understand that he was right.

Greed is simply the willingness to line your own pockets at someone else's expense. Extreme measures to accomplish that collection of wealth are common place. Just look at Africa. What Africa needs more than H.I.V. drugs, international investment or debt relief is leaders who are not corrupt. Over the decades, how many billions of dollars have been yanked away from the inhabitants of the poorest continent on earth by leaders who used their political power to cut up the financial cake for themselves? How much international relief money has been diverted from poor people and ended up in Swiss bank accounts? This is theft, pure and simple.

Throughout history religion has been used to facilitate theft. Once the church becomes contaminated by political power the rape of the average citizen begins. Perhaps the most blatant example of unrelenting greed was pulled off by the Catholic Church and the Spanish monarchy. The Inquisition was religious terrorism of the highest order. If you stepped outside the accepted beliefs of the day you were tortured until you recanted; then you were either murdered or released. This wasn't just a temporary glitch in religious behavior. The inquisition went on for centuries. Why then was this religious nightmare allowed to continue for such a long time? One would think that people of good conscience would certainly bring the slaughter to a halt. The simple answer is that the inquisition was profitable. No matter whether the grand inquisitor killed or released you, your property was confiscated. You can imagine how much wealth could be accumulated over hundreds of years by simply targeting the right people. The church just had to hire a few sadists who they knew would enjoy their work and let the plunder begin.

By contrast, the Salem witch trials lasted only 16 months. That's because there was no money to be made by hanging witches. Had there been a thousand dollar bounty on witches, in all probability witch hunting groups would still be active in Massachusetts today.

It's difficult to separate greed from the lust for power. Money is power. You can't launch a military machine without adequate funding. But for the sake of clarity let's approach power as a separate subject from greed. Power is the ability to make people do what you want them to do. If you are charismatic and really good at manipulating the masses, then religious power struggles will go your way. As your power base becomes more secure, you can then systematically crush all expression of criticism and resistance. The unbelievers (uncooperative) must be purged in order for your movement to thrive. The trick is to get the masses to dance to your tune, and that's where terror plays a big part. Going back to the Inquisition, can you imagine stepping out of line knowing that you would face the torturers as a result?

Besides terrifying the masses half to death, making them feel good (or justified) also contributes to the desired effect. Hitler was a genius when it came to whipping up enthusiasm. You are the Master Race. You will inherit the world. It is your birth right. Religion simply adds "You are doing the will of God" to this feel good approach. A few initial successes and the momentum builds. After all, if your conquests grow larger and larger, it must be the will of God. Now you have the full attention of the masses. There is nothing like being on a winning team. Everyone seems to fall in line and ambiguity is deleted. Power then grows as the number of followers hanging on your every word increases. A religious leader who has a thousand followers waving swords over their heads is ten times as powerful as a religious leader with only a hundred sword waving followers. The goal simply becomes the multiplication of the flock. Violent religious leaders have no interest in listening to anything that will diminish the number of their followers.

On the other hand the followers themselves don't want to stop waving their swords. Sword waving provides a genuine rush. What a sense of empowerment, just like the gunslingers of the old west. That's why if a religious leader with a hundred sword waving followers suddenly started preaching religious tolerance, the sword wavers would pause for a moment, stare at each other, scratch their heads and run and join the group that has a thousand sword waving followers. After all, why lose momentum?

Of all people, it was George Carlin who pointed out that everyone who has preached religious tolerance on a grand scale has been murdered. Ghandi, Christ, Martin Luther King junior, etc. etc. etc., all dead. Carlin's conclusion is that we are not ready for that kind of thinking. However you perceive George's rantings, he was absolutely right on this point. We are still cave men with a very thin veneer of civilization. We are dangerous.

Another significant source of religious violence is psychiatric illness. True psychosis is a terrifying disease. In an exacerbation of schizophrenia your personality literally starts to dissolve. Where do you run when the core of who you are is falling apart? As a Physician's Assistant I used to work at a local mid west airport. We saw a lot of psychotics. A colleague of mind postulated that the psychotic feels that they might get better if they could only change their location. As a result, they would try to run away from their own mental illness and end up at the airport. A woman wearing three sunglasses walked up to the Allegheny Airlines ticket booth and demanded a personal helicopter escort to LaGuardia. After being called, I gently intervened along with two huge state cops. She told the admitting physician in the psychiatric unit that at first she thought I looked like Jesus. But after a while she figured out that I was part of the plot against her.

I remember two other psychotics each of whom were escorted to my airport office on separate occasions. Even though these psychotics did not know each other, their stories were identical. They both complained about being sexually assaulted by laser beams emitting from water pipes in their houses. I went home after these episodes being very glad that most of my plumbing was below ground.

Most psychotics are harmless, but they are terrified by the voices screaming in their head. The voices themselves are a fascinating phenomena. Where do they come from? You can understand why ancient people thought psychosis was the result of demonic possession. How else could you explain voices coming out of nowhere that cause the psychotic fear and delusions?

One young lady came to my emergency room late at night. She was a psychotic with a rare gift. She had insight into her disease. She said "The voices are telling me to do bad things to myself. I'm scared! I need to be in a safe place." Her eyes were filled with tears. I thought that was one of the most honest statements I had ever heard. I got on the phone and spent ninety minutes moving heaven and earth to get her an emergency psychiatric bed that night.

As I said, most psychotics are harmless and can be helped by medication. The voices have to be organic in origin, otherwise the appropriate pills wouldn't make the voices go away. But occasionally you do get the paranoid schizophrenic. They think you are trying to kill them and will do anything to protect themselves. Never get between them and the door and never let them get between you and the door. If you find yourself standing in a doorway looking at someone on the ground bleeding from a stab wound, do not enter that room before checking all four corners of the room. You are looking for someone who is playing with a knife, pacing about in an agitated manner and carrying on an intense conversation with a person or persons who are invisible. Those voices are telling him that you are part of Satan's plot against him. Back off and wait for the cops.

On occasion you can see a psychotic on the lockup ward spending endless amounts of time with an old well used Bible. Every page of that bible will have almost microscopic notations in the margins cross-referencing one bible verse with another. Psychotics are attracted to religion because it provides structure for their disintegrating personalities. Psychosis creates internal chaos. The delusional voices unhinge those poor souls from any consistent reality. They desperately hang onto religion as a reliable foundation. Any port in a storm, and an exacerbation of psychosis is a true storm.

There is another very interesting aspect to a psychotic's thought processes. Their thinking tends to be very literal. When they are in the throes of their illness abstraction becomes difficult. I have asked psychotics "You have heard of the saying 'People who live in glass houses shouldn't throw stones'. What do you think that saying means"? The literal answer comes back "The glass breaks". Although the tendency toward literal thinking is not universal, it is a predictable trend.

There are many different levels of schizophrenia. Some people fall under the classification of a borderline schizophrenic personality. Those folk never end up on a psychiatric lock up ward. They are just a bit odd, keep pretty much to themselves and occasionally stare into space. They hold down simple jobs and just get on with their lives. But occasionally a borderline psychotic or perhaps manic depressive is charismatic and a good public speaker. People start to listen to them. The flock begins to form. Once in a while you can have the privilege of watching a TV evangelist descend into frank psychosis. That really hurts their fund raising efforts. But if a borderline psychotic can keep it together enough to form a group of followers, trouble often erupts. I cannot prove this, but it makes sense to me that the literal thinking of the psychotic patient could give rise to the very inflexible code of a cult. Furthermore, if that revered religious leader has the occasional psychotic delusion which his followers interpret as a revelation, then real trouble erupts. The followers will carry out the instructions of that epiphany no matter how much chaos and carnage results. How could they be wrong? After all, the revelation came from God.

Jones Town and Waco are prime examples of the result of a psychotic leader's delusions. I really believe that David Koresh in Waco thought that setting his religious compound ablaze was going to be the initiating event of the Apocalypse described in the book of Revelations. A lot of his followers, including children, paid a huge price for his delusions. In Jones Town the cult leader's psychotic delusions led to a group poisoning. The really scary thing is that when he gave the order for the mass suicide, over a hundred people not only killed themselves, but their own children as well. The fact that he had adequate cyanide available to do the job tells you that, from the beginning, he knew he was leading his followers to a mini Armageddon.

As a footnote, and having nothing to do with religion, I once worked with a delightful schizophrenic while I was a medical student. The patient's condition had greatly improved with his medications and he was going to be discharged soon from our psychiatric ward. In the outside world, he was a very good mathematician. He would complete a year long university mathematics course in three months. Psychotics are often very intelligent. Towards the end of his hospital stay Andrew asked me to give an honest answer to a question. I said "Sure, what's the question?" He said "The other day I asked one of the nurses to give me an electric razor so that I could shave. I wanted to use the mirror attached to that wall over there. The nearest electrical outlet is five feet away from the mirror. The cord on the electric razor is four feet long". I said "So what's the question?" He said, "Have I been secretly enrolled in a hospital study on how human beings respond to frustration?"

Leaving the issue of psychosis for a moment, religion has a way of making people do things that are both unnatural and unhealthy. The man who drew the original blueprint for Christian theology, Paul the apostle, had a problem. He was consumed with Christ. He found that his earthly needs diminished his focus and energy for his spiritual tasks, so he drew visual images in his letters of his spirit warring against his flesh, "Oh wretched man that I am... etc. etc". Christianity has being pursuing mortification of the flesh ever since. To suffer is to love God. Our mortal urges (i.e. sexual drive) have to be conquered for us to be pure and focused on spiritual matters. As a result, nuns and priests give up sex and family forever. There are monasteries where the monks not only take a vow of silence; they are not even allowed to make eye contact with each other. Monks have also been known to physically torture themselves in order to subdue their earthly desires. I am sure there are people on this planet who gain spiritual insight as a result of a period of isolation or abstinence. But as a general philosophy this is an unbelievably twisted way to live. It makes for bitterness, and the pain of knowing that you've missed the best parts of life. I would suggest that the most effective way to convert people to your faith is to have a genuine smile on your face and a sense of inner peace and well being. You have to lead a balanced life to achieve those qualities. Your needs are just as important as the needs of anyone else in your religious community. Fundamental to this concept is the awareness that one fulfillment is not meant to substitute for another. There's time for both the spirit and the flesh. But here is my real heresy. The spirit and the flesh can actually augment each other. I honestly believe that the division we have made between the spirit and the flesh is a useless concept. A great sexual experience can be so powerful that it can lead you to the nether regions of your own soul. One of life's greatest gifts is to be able to let go completely. A Methodist minister friend of mine called this act of total release "abandonment". What a gift to be that connected. But that's too much out of control for most religious leaders. For them there really is such a thing as too much fun. Religious leaders know how powerful the sexual drive is, thus they figure if they can control someone's sexual drive, they can control the person. The way they gain that control is truly sinister. The religious leader will tell the novitiate that the only way they can give up sex and family forever is to love God more than anything else. The question then becomes "Do you love God enough to make that commitment?" If you don't love God enough, you can go your own way; but in the back of your mind you know you are a religious loser. You were unable to rise to the spiritual challenge.

But there's an additional issue. Not only is abstinence from normal sexual relations a formula for bitterness and regret, it attracts perverts. Think about it. As a Catholic priest you get to wear a dress, have nothing intimate to do with women, live with other men and have unlimited access to children. This is not rocket science. Is anyone surprised about the thousands of sexual assault cases emerging involving priests and children? Read about what happened to children in Catholic institutions in Ireland during the 20th Century as documented by "The Commission to Inquire into Child Abuse", which was released in 2009. The contents of that report will make you truly ill. What's even worse, the perpetrators of those crimes won immunity from the Irish courts, so no one can be prosecuted. Where is the justice? What further befuddles me is the Catholic hierarchy moving pedophiles from one unsuspecting parish to another so they wouldn't get caught. Why isn't the act of hiding sexual predators prosecuted as obstruction of justice? And why was the religious hierarchy so protective of the pedophile in the first place? Well, does anyone really believe that the priesthood's tendency towards sexual predatory behavior just started with our generation?

Speaking for the opposition, "too much fun" can lead to unwanted pregnancy, gonorrhea, syphilis, chlamydia (with the resulting infertility), herpes, HIV, hepatitis B, hepatitis C, cervical cancer and death, just to name a few. In addition, not having family ties has left priests and nuns free to serve in truly god forsaken parts of the planet. They are not afraid to take that huge and dangerous risk.

The bottom line is that there is no one spiritual track for everyone. But as religious people we do have the right and obligation to step back and try to learn from what we observe. We have to be open to better ideas. I am convinced that as human beings we were meant to enrich each other's lives. It's a gift and something to be celebrated.

Years ago I had the privilege of visiting the German city of Trier. It was at one time among the largest cities in the world and the seat of Constantine's Roman Empire. There is one original Roman gate still standing in that city. The brilliance of the defensive technology in that gate is obvious. At some point in the middle ages the local leadership decided to incorporate the solid stone structure of that gate into one wall of a new church. As they were building the church, one monk asked if he could be placed inside the church's wall. He would have one tiny room with only one small slit to the outside world through which local folk would pass food and water. There wasn't any door, so he could never leave. He wanted to do this so that he could completely devote himself to contemplating and worshiping God. The authorities granted his request. For years, the offered food and water disappeared into the slit. Eventually, passersby heard unremitting mumbling coming from the chamber. After a while that mumbling progressed to constant screaming which eventually led to total silence. This is the natural effect of years of solitary confinement on a human being.

The only good news is that because of the piety of his religious request, some idiot proclaimed him a saint. The rules of the day said that you cannot tear down the tomb of a saint; thus the Roman gate still stands intact for all to see and appreciate. The monk is still inside the church's wall, a monument to mortification of the flesh.

ON RELIGION Part B

In the final analysis, the most critical choice people face with regard to religion is the choice between rationality and insanity. If we choose the aspects of any religion that have, under strict unrelenting scrutiny over time, improved the lot of humanity and the collective richness of our lives, then we have a cause for affirmation. If we choose the crazy aspects of religion, then we reap the inevitable outcome, which is human suffering and slaughter. The simple trick is to be able to see the difference between religious rationality and mental instability. The emotional frenzy of religion tends to blur that distinction. As a starting point, if you want to track down the crazy side of religion, just follow the trail of blood.

As a child I remember sitting in a church camp and joyfully singing "Joshua fought the battle of Jericho and the walls came a tumbling down". The song had a really bouncy rhythm. We clapped our hands, occasionally throwing in bits of harmony. What I am curious about is why there wasn't a happy verse about the slaughter that occurred after the walls fell. According to the Bible, every citizen of Jericho was "put to the edge of the sword", in other words hacked to pieces, except for a prostitute who helped some Israeli spies. Somehow as church going kids we disconnected from the bloodletting. How did we do that? The answer is that the slaughter was simply never addressed as an issue. After all, the good guys won.

I am sorry folks, but Joshua goes through the Promised Land like Attila the Hun. When the Israelites conquered a regional tribe, they killed everyone, occasionally sparing some virgins. Theologians can always find a few good reasons to spare virgins. But why were these massacres seen as acceptable? The answer was simple. As the Bible says "God has given them into your hand". Once again the green light had been given for religious ethnic cleansing. When you see a comment like

"God has given them into your hand" it usually meant that someone at the time felt bad about committing mass murder. But the religious historians made it all better, as they always do.

Why did God want the original inhabitants of the Promised Land exterminated? Because "The Lord your God is a jealous God." Yahweh was afraid the Israelites would worship the idols of the indigenous peoples. So rather than have the religious purity of the Israelites compromised, the conquered nations had to be wiped off the face of the earth. I don't get it. What has the creator of the universe got to feel jealous about? I understand that the Old Testament is the history of an ancient people hammering out their religious identity. I also understand that ancient tribes were not interested in gods that would not help them win wars. But the God of the Pentateuch is a vain monster. He wants the undying worship and obedience of his chosen people. Toward that end, Yahweh is willing to use the Israelites to commit genocide throughout the Promised Land. This is just one more example of the chosen killing the unchosen.

Let's leave the Old Testament for a moment and turn to the Bhagavad Gita, the holy script of the Hindu faith. One of the Bhagavad Gita's central stories revolves around a character named Arjuna. Arjuna is a revered warrior and unbeatable with a bow and arrow. He is such a great warrior that he has his own chariot and chariot driver. As time goes by, Arjuna becomes friends with his chariot driver. The two of them eventually find themselves on the front line of a major battle just before it begins. Arjuna looks across at the enemy line and sees close family members that he has known his whole life. He knows that in a few minutes he will be called upon to put arrows into those relatives. He expresses his sincere misgivings to his chariot driver.

Upon reading the Bhagavad Gita for the first time I thought, "At last we are going to get some solid religious insight into preventing violence!" But wait! The chariot driver is no ordinary chariot driver. Before Arjuna's eyes his driver transforms into the great god Krishna who then begins an elaborate monologue about how Arjuna must set his concerns for his relatives to one side. Krishna *wants* the war to happen. In fact, Krishna has already determined the battle's outcome. All that remains to be done is the actual slaughter itself. Krishna goes on to explain how the eternal soul cannot be killed. Whenever someone dies, his eternal soul just moves onto the next reincarnation. Therefore, since the soul is immortal, Arjuna's family members will not really come to the end of their existence. Having thus attenuated Arjuna's concerns, Krishna then leads Arjuna into the fray.

Notice how the above story demonstrates the same kind of other world thinking that we have just discussed. Simply put, the concept of the afterlife (or next reincarnation) determines what is morally acceptable in the present. In fact, all of the major religions with blood on their hands place such emphasis on the eternal soul, that concerns for our transient mortal lives pale by comparison. This almost universal disregard for human suffering is a direct result of the collective stampede for immortality. Such an inflexible and sterile disconnect, I would also argue, is at least partially a result of the religious believer's desire to conquer the yearnings of the flesh. Hitting the big "Off" switch to one's emotions is the only way Christians could have committed unspeakable acts in torture chambers upon unbelievers in the middle ages. In short, our belief systems have turned us into something less than human. After all, if God is willing to burn us in hell for all eternity, what does it then matter if we do something similar in order to save the unbeliever's soul?

Turning the page to another major religion, I don't have to look in the Koran for verses that condone religious violence. Muslim extremists are currently as violent as anyone in religious history. This kind of behavior would not be surprising in the dark or middle ages, but in the twenty first century?!? Have we learned nothing from our past? But wait a minute. It's all O.K. This time Allah has set us on the one true path.

Much has been said and written about the rise of Islamic religious extremism. Without question it's a complicated subject. But whatever is said, whatever words are used to discuss the matter, never take your eyes off the results of their work. The result of their work is the mass murder of civilians. Don't allow any lofty concepts to obscure that truth.

Even the term "religious extremist" is misleading. Ultra Orthodox Jews are religious extremists, but the resulting bloodshed these days is nothing when compared to their Old Testament history. Rabid born again Christians are religious extremists but currently their violence is limited to social bigotry and the occasional snake bite (no recent lynchings). Even the Amish are religious extremists. Their code is so rigid they don't even use electricity. But you rarely see a horse drawn buggy packed with dynamite deliberately being driven into a market place.

The term "Islamic extremist" misses the point. The proper name for people who do what radical Islamists are now doing is "Islamic murderers". But the religious apologists will do all they can to obscure that reality. All sorts of justifications, and all in the name of Allah, will be given to smoke screen their carnage. It all has to be justified, otherwise it is murder and the violent Islamic leaders know that.

If you wade through some of the Islamic hatred that spews forth from their pulpits, you will hear the frequent claim that Islam is under attack. No, Islam is not under attack. What is under attack is the idea that you can violently impose Sharia law on cultures that don't want it. That is under attack.

You also hear how violent Islam is a justified response to Western religious aggression. The terrorists are still angry about the Crusades. Granted the Crusades were criminal, but here is the real irony. The violence of the Islamic extremists has made them the crusaders of the twenty first century. They have become what they say they hate the most.

Violent Islamic extremism has another downside. It attracts serial killers. Just like pedophiles are drawn to the priesthood, serial killers gravitate to the bloodletting. Instead of being hunted by the law, the serial killer is now a hero in his local peer group. It was obvious that al Zarqawi in Iraq and several others were enjoying the beheadings just a bit too much. Recently a video emerged of a twelve year old boy being guided through a beheading. The motivations behind that horrendous act have nothing to do with religion. In another case, one extremist prides himself in throwing the first stone at a stoning. Do you think this guy has issues?

A few years ago terrorists in Northern Pakistan started to target doctors, which tells you exactly how much the Islamic fascists care about the regional population. It was undoubtedly part of a program to destabilize the local society. Terrorists thrive in social chaos. I remember one gut wrenching story of a young Pakistani doctor who trained in the United States. He could have stayed in the USA and made good money, but he wanted to go back to Pakistan to help his people. He was a man of good conscience. One day on the way to work, someone on a motorcycle pulled up next to him and blew his brains out. Now let's think about this. It took that physician a minimum of twenty three years of education (probably more if he trained in both Pakistan and the United States) to give him the skills and qualifications necessary to practice responsible medicine. It took one easily led lunatic less than a few seconds to blow all of that knowledge out of his head. But let's push the issue even further. Let's do some math. During my career in the emergency room I saw about three thousand patients a year. However in the third world you can see people much more rapidly than I could because you don't have to wait for the results of elaborate blood tests, x-rays, c.t. scans etc. etc. So a very conservative estimate would be that this physician could have seen about five thousand Pakistani patients a year. For the sake of argument, let's say that he would have practiced twenty five more years had he not been shot. His death meant that about one hundred and twenty five thousand patient visits will not happen. One could argue that other doctors will step in and see those patients. But by the time this particular wave of terrorism ended about seventy doctors were dead. Using the same approximate numbers, that means eight million seven hundred and fifty thousand patient visits will not happen. How many children died as a result of the lack of medical care, we will never know. What kind of God is glorified by this kind of behavior? Why not just offer the children up as human sacrifices? The end result is the same.

Religious extremists have also come up with an interesting approach to rape. In order for a man to be convicted of rape in a tribal Islamic court, there have to be four witnesses to that rape. But wait, it gets better. Women only count as half a witness. This is the same thinking that made blacks one third of a man for purposes of the population census during the years of slavery in the United States. Eight women witnesses would be strong enough to pull the attacker off the victim. So requiring eight women witnesses to prosecute a rape case is meaningless. But it gets better still. Infidels, stain on the earth that we are, don't count as witnesses. Therefore a tour bus can pull up alongside the rape, and it will be as if the rape never happened.

Every society has its share of sexual predators. If you make rape unpunishable (and therefore a man's right) serial rapists will migrate to that area the same way that pedophiles are drawn to South East Asia.

I cannot get out of my mind the tragic story of a young woman in

Pakistan. Walking along one day, she had a conversation with a boy she knew from her village. For religious and cultural reasons, the two of them talking together in public was forbidden. She was brought before the Islamic village elders. The girl's father argued that the boy had not yet reached sexual maturity, so sexual impropriety wasn't even possible. The girl defended herself by saying that she regularly taught the Koran in the local school. But a line had been crossed and someone had to pay. In these cultures it is usually the woman who pays. So the village elders decided to have her serially raped by four local dirt bags. For her, this is a near death sentence. Not only does she have to live with the trauma of multiple rapes and possible pregnancy (imagine what happens to *that* child), but she has been defiled. She can never have a husband or legitimate family. Finally the Pakistani government stepped in and arrested the rapists.

In 2002, a very disturbing story emerged from Saudi Arabia. Fourteen school girls were trapped inside their school which had accidentally caught fire. The fire brigade arrived and began organizing a rescue operation. Then the religious police arrived and determined that the girls inside the burning school did not have appropriate garb with them to be seen in public. Therefore the religious police prevented the firemen from rescuing the school girls. The school girls burned to death.

I've taken care of burn patients, and it is without question the most painful injury anyone can have. There are countless nerve endings in the skin and in a serious burn every one of those nerve endings is screaming. But wait. Everything is fine. Allah will reward those girls in the afterlife. How sick does it have to get? How much collective cruelty do we have to endure?

Two of the finest medical minds I know are both women. Under radical Islam those women and many like them would never be allowed to pursue a medical career. In that culture women are fit to study only the Koran.

Have you noticed that cultures that condone violent religious extremism tend to degrade and control women? That's a general trend, with a few violent and bigoted European Queens being very notable exceptions. "Bloody Mary" of England was called that for very good reasons. Queen Isabella I of Spain was a driving force behind the Inquisition. True bigotry knows no gender boundaries. But it is consistently predictable that a violent religious culture will be male dominant. That's because women have a more nurturing quality than men (again with notable exceptions). When women have a strong voice within society they tend to have a breaking action on unlimited bloodshed. For instance, it was the mothers of Northern Ireland that finally put the peace process on a solid footing. They simply got tired of watching their sons die.

You have to admit that the call to righteousness and salvation is a very powerful and seductive force. It is the power base of, and to some extent defines and reinforces the religious elite's own identify. All a Priest, Rabbi Minister or Imam have to do to remain on top of the religious food chain is to act out their role in a convincing manner. If you entertain dark thoughts or fuck choir boys behind closed doors, who's to know?

In all fairness, there are aesthetic branches of Islam that affirm the value of human life. But you can take the most benign religion in the world, place that religion in the wrong hands and heads will roll. For example, Christ's general approach to existence was non violent. But for centuries, certain groups of Christians were major league killers.

In a slightly more benign form, ultra conservative theology leads to what I will call "theological wishful thinking". There's a tremendous driving tendency within people to tie up all the loose ends in their particular theological construct. The creation mythology of Genesis might be literally true if only evolution of the species, carbon dating and the findings of geology and paleontology did not exist. Make no mistake about it, there are people who are still searching for the Garden of Eden and Noah's Ark. I remember as a child being ushered through the supermarket checkout line and past the tabloids. One tabloid front page contained a photograph of a few old pieces of wood scattered on a barren mountain top, followed by the large headline "Noah's Ark found!" It was right next to the article on the alien space child being discovered on a Nebraska farm (complete with photographs).

So the religious delight experienced when one seems to be dealing with an ironclad theological belief system can only be sustained by talking to people who all think in exactly the same way. This leads to a very defensive posturing. The insecurity inherent in an unquestioning faith often leads to a violent response to those who see things differently.

We've discussed at length the tension that exists between the saved and the unsaved. All I am asking for is the realization that if you live within an inflexible religious belief system, your apparent joy at having all the answers sits upon a very shaky foundation. As a result you will feel anger towards anyone who challenges your cherished theology.

I remember sitting in a bible study years ago. One young earnest believer emphatically stated that God would surround him with good people in the afterlife because he himself had forgiven those who had wronged him on earth. Sounds good. I sat there for a while and caught his vibes. I finally said "You're full of anger". The bible study came to a grinding halt. After all, true born agains who have filled themselves with the spirit of Christ shouldn't be full of anger. But his anger was palpable. Instead of seeing that anger as a pathway to further growth, the group became uncomfortable with my questions. I had exposed the tension that exists between who we really are and what our religion allows us to be. It was time for me to go.

Going once again back to my youth, I went to Church every Sunday and confessed my sins and failings. After our confession, the Minister would reassure us that we were forgiven. Following that reassurance, the choir would sing and we were asked for money. After a while I concluded that this approach to religion was really self defeating. We always failed and fell short of the glory of God, but the perfect God always forgave us. Providing that window for forgiveness gave the church a very powerful hold over the believers. Personally, I couldn't wait for Monday so I could go out and fail again. One of the most intelligent comments on religion that I've ever heard was originally said by an old friend of mine while we were still both in high school. One day John turned to me and said "What kind of God would condemn people for doing the extremely predictable things they do?" That's a very good question.

In a certain sense, the longer religion keeps hammering away at our shortcomings, the weaker we get. No one seems to have asked the simple question "What makes people grow?" Instead of focusing on our failings, how about asking our religion to affirm our humanity? How about celebrating and being grateful for our lives? Almost any strong emotion can be an opportunity for growth. Taking this approach necessitates the willingness to explore the darker recesses of our own souls. Those darker recesses exist for a reason. Often, with little effort, we can come through that darkness and emerge as much stronger human beings. As a result, we can actually heal ourselves, and that is a gift.

If you are a rapist or beat your wife or commit felonies, then you have reasons to feel guilty. What's really scary is that those with truly antisocial personalities feel no guilt. All that matters to them is how things affect them directly. But greater than ninety five percent of the population isn't like that. The vast majority of people want to go to work and raise their kids in a proper manner. If your religion always makes you feel bad about who you are, your personal growth will stop. You'll just run in the same guilt ridden religious endless loop. How about a message from the pulpit that simply says "You and I are accepted". Imagine the doors that would open.

Returning to the subject of religious violence, the British newspapers have recently focused on a conservative branch of Islam called Tablighi Jamaat. This movement originally rose out of the Deopandi theology which arose from Sunni Islam. It is full of hatred for the "Kuffar" (non Muslim) in Western civilization. Granted, there is a lot of Western civilization that needs rejecting. Our young people are being raised in a moral vacuum. Their day to day lives have been reduced to flashing lights and sound bites. I remember turning on the television and watching a video where a black rapper brags about doing his bitch in the back seat of his limousine. What is a young child supposed to do with those images?

So, our cultural priorities have indeed been turned upside down by the "anything for a buck" mentality. Ethical and religious people have a right to be upset over our children being spoon fed pure brainless garbage. However that problem isn't solved by becoming a "hater". When you mix hate with religious zeal then, once again, the bloodletting begins. Take a good hard look at the Middle East. As of this writing (September 07) the Palestinian problem is still not solved. Hamas and Habas are at each other's throats. Diplomacy seems to be a completely lost art. Hezbollah is at war with Israel and Lebanese Christians. Syria and Iran are pouring men and munitions into that conflict. Sunnis and Shiites are killing each other. In Southern Iraq even rival Shiite groups are at war. And finally the chronic smouldering war between Muslims and Hindus flares up periodically. Just recently, Hindus started killing Christians.

For a moment, let's put all the complicated historical and political issues to one side. Where's the hope? Where is the real path to a lasting peace? Perhaps the protagonists simply aren't tired of killing each other. After all, if you have been a militant your whole life what are you going to do for a living when the shooting stops?

In Palestine there is somewhere a young woman who has two fine sons aged eight and ten. We'll call one son Habib and the other Mohammed. Both boys are intelligent. Both do well in school and honor their parents. They are the kind of youngsters every family hopes for. Both boys decide to continue their education and become professionals. They are the apple of their mother's eye. She loves them deeply.

But late at night while everyone is asleep the young mother lays awake, stares at the ceiling and worries. What are the odds that her boys will live to fulfill their dreams? Will they get lucky and continue their education, or will they fall under the influence of a "Hater"? Will they provide critically needed help to rebuild their society, or will they become forgotten statistics. Will they one day get talked into strapping dynamite around their waist or will they become the true diplomats so desperately needed? Will they die under an Israeli air strike, or even worse, join separate sectarian groups and end up shooting each other? Of course, prior to becoming a martyr, they will be promised endless rewards in heaven. The family will also experience the prestige of having given up their sons for Islam. The dead sons will then be enshrined within religious rhetoric. But the young mother cannot sleep. In the distance there is gun fire. A tear runs down her cheek. Her son's own her heart.

Within the complex cauldron of the Middle East, only one thing remains certain. If you teach your kids to hate, war will find its way to your doorstep again and again.

The unrelenting carnage that results from religious rhetoric being infused into our fundamentally violent and flawed nature leads me to postulate two general rules that should be applied to all religions:

Rule No.1: It is not permissible to torture or kill another human being for no other reason than the fact that they belong to a religion or sect outside of your own. The second rule follows from the first:

Rule No.2: No religious belief or edict is more important than another human being. Even now I can hear the Bible belters beating their breasts crying out "This is Humanism!" No, this is called compassion. Without compassion as its corner stone, any religion has the potential to become the devil's best work.

These two rules are not hard to understand. Any grade school kid can grasp these simple concepts. But such guidelines will never be applied to most of the world's religions. Too many people are in love with their hatred. It keeps them warm at night and gives them a sense of purpose and identity.

I was sitting at the breakfast table finishing up my tea and toast when I commented to my wife about the latest religious atrocity mentioned in the newspaper. She paused for minute, put down her cup of tea, turned to me and came up with one of her not infrequent profound comments. She said "If there is a heaven, I know what question the gatekeeper will ask those who wish to enter". I said, "Well, what is that question?" She replied, "While looking the person who wishes to enter heaven right in the eye, the keeper of the heavenly gate will ask, 'During your time on earth, how many tears did you cause to be shed?' If the number of tears resulting from that person's life on earth turns out to be a large number, they will not be allowed into heaven."

Chapter VIII

ON THE WAY TO CARBON

England 2007

It's late September. Winds are howling through my little eighteenth century English village. That village sits on top of an exposed plateau which makes the village dwellers feel the power of the wind more than those living in the surrounding lowlands. Today's winds are unusually cold for this time of year. Summer has not even officially come to an end, but when I walked outside to get something out of the car I could see my breath. Fortunately, the blazing fire in my metal backed Victorian fireplace provides comforting warmth. Standing outside our dining room, the dog has his face plastered against the glass patio door. His current patrol has confirmed that none of the neighbor's dogs or cats have invaded our property boundaries. Duty thus fulfilled, he has no intention of staying out in that wind any longer than absolutely necessary.

Sitting in front of the fire, my mind wanders back to my seminary days. It's difficult to believe that those classes occurred thirty five years ago. Where did the time go?

What specifically comes to mind is a special class coordinated by Professor Tom Driver. One day, Tom stood up and presented the class with a question. He asked "What is your primary religious symbol?" As most of the students put their heads down and pondered the issue, a spontaneous image flashed into my consciousness. That image showed a fireplace which contained a roaring fire. Within a few moments I realized that any such fire would draw people closer to it. A fire is warm, inviting, and has a way of creating a community. Get good people together around a fireplace, sprinkle lightly with wine and it's a no lose situation. Smiles will abound and good memories will be created.

Partly as a result of my innate lingering fear of individual contact and partly because of my love of teaching and public speaking, I always found groups of good hearted folk a joy. All I ask of group members is that they be able to listen as well as verbalize. True openness requires the ability to give and take.

Thus the fireplace symbol became the foundation for my religious approach to life. That symbol helped me to appreciate, despite all our individual craziness, the richness of our common human experience. With a bit of pure luck, as well as hard won insight, life can be a joy.

So, what about my own relationship to a deity? This question presents dangerous ground for me as religious clichés from the past move in from the surrounding darkness. But I do owe an answer to that difficult question after having just written page after page poking holes in people's cherished religious icons. So, with all appropriate humility, here goes.

I am a theist. I can't help it; it's in my blood. Out of the vapors of my late teenage years I began having religious experiences. I did not have any audio or visual hallucinations, flight of ideas, pressured speech, abuse drugs or alcohol, take any medications, stare into space, or make small children nervous. Instead I experienced a sudden and unexpected presence that was full of energy and warmth. It came out of nowhere. Granted, I was under the influence of a very powerful church based youth movement at that time. For years the church provided a framework for my experiences and I believed that traditional theology hook, line and sinker. But as my experiences grew and matured I was drawn away from the church and deeper into the rich connections between good people. I have seen that richness and energy in Protestants, Catholics, Jews, Hindus, Buddhists and Muslims. The people who impress me the most are those who will do the right thing in any given situation, not because their religion demands that they do it, but because they know that it's just the right thing to do. That combination of conviction, insight and caring crosses all religious boundaries. No one religion has an exclusive claim to God. The creator of the universe is much too all encompassing for that.

I clearly realized that my belief in a deity flies in the face of most of the facts gathered by objective and critical observations. All you have to do is watch lions bring down a zebra, or watch a child die of a slowly progressive brain tumor to realize that no compassionate entity is in charge of this planet. Although our earth is a true oasis in the darkness of space, it is also a brutal place built on the principle of eat or be eaten. For example, as you are reading this, you are being attacked by bacteria and viruses. Fortunately you have an immune system that is capable of fighting off the infectious invasion, for now. But you are constantly under the threat of extinction.

The natural evil we experience every day in life is not the result of Eve eating the apple. Earthquakes, plagues, tsunamis etc. are all there by design. It's almost as if our individual existences have been set adrift in a milieu of consistent physical laws. We careen through life, sometimes making good, sometimes bad decisions. But no matter what our individual circumstances, we are all extremely vulnerable.

Medicine provided me with an avenue to minister to that vulnerability which bypassed religiosity completely. What a relief. I would pray with people if they asked me to, but I never tried to put any of my religious baggage on them. As I said before, with the assistance of good medical intervention, people heal themselves.

Despite my rejection of the church, I am still drawn to the figure of Christ. Regardless of all the historical uncertainty, there is in the synoptic gospels (Mathew, Mark and Luke) the imprint of an immensely creative mind that was light years ahead of his and our time. What draws me most strongly to Christ's words is his sense of decency. The story of the Good Samaritan, the Beatitudes, and the story of the woman caught in adultery just do it for me. I don't need the miracles, many of which were probably later additions to prove Christ's divinity. Remember, every candidate for sainthood needs at least two confirmed miracles.

So, is Christ the son of God? I haven't the faintest idea. But although it's heresy, I can still love him and leave that question unanswered. I have my own given religious pathway and it's a good place to be.

When I was struggling with career options, I took part in a volunteer public work's project in the Bay Islands off Honduras. While I was there the Honduran physician who ran the Island's clinic had to go to the mainland for a government meeting. That left me with my physician's assistant training and some good nurses medically in charge of the Island's population. In the United States this would never be possible. The nurses and I were truly on our own.

One day an elderly black man dressed formally in a suit and tie (despite the baking afternoon sun) made his way to our clinic. He wanted to pick up some medications for his house bound wife. She had diabetes and congestive heart failure. Some of what he said didn't make sense to me so I decided it was time to make a house call. After the clinic closed I followed him up Goat Hill to meet his wife Miss Matilda. She was lying in her bed in a small wooden room, lit only by one tiny window. Her medical situation was not good and she knew it. But she patted the Bible on her chest. Whatever happened to her, she had her Jesus. There was however, something very special about Miss Matilda. An energy emitted from her that filled that dark room. She looked me straight in the eye and said "When are you going to come and build a hospital on this island? It will be too late for me, but there will be others who will come after me." I had no answer to her question, but her wonderful presence never left me.

Regrettably I never returned to the island of Roatan. A few weeks after meeting Ms Matilda I bid a fond farewell to the good Mormons who ran the public health project in which we worked. I flew home to Indiana, closed my small business (that was going nowhere) and went to medical school.

Chapter IX

M.S.65

After leaving direct sales I opened a rare coin store. Again, why not? My father started me collecting coins at the age of five. I still remember in 1952, a 1940 proof set that my father had ordered from a dealer arriving in the mail. I still have it. I was immediately addicted. I spent hours poring over penny rolls and trying to get relatives to back my rare coin purchases.

In later life I found the hobby relaxed me. I could be attributing die varieties of United States large cents and a bomb could go off two blocks away and I wouldn't hear it. I was totally immersed in my treasure hunt. So when my dear maiden aunt passed away and left me $18,000, I opened the store. It was a small time operation. I catered to the average collector; people who shared my obsession.

As a group, coin collectors can be odd ducks. Sitting at home fondling pieces of metal can be a way of not dealing with the world. But a lot of coin collectors are also very intelligent people. Once you get done talking about coins, you might find other facets of their lives and expertise that are worth exploring. Any good hobby just makes life more interesting. For example I learned a bit about sailing from one of my customers and he got caught up with my interest in emergency medicine. I ended up training him as an Emergency Medical Technician and I made several voyages on his sail boat. I filled my coin store with overstuffed chairs and people would stop in just to spend the afternoon. A good time was had by all.

The back wall of the store separated my business from a small apartment. A young couple rented that apartment. Our shared wall was just sheet rock, so any loud noise from the apartment could easily be heard in the store. This couple seemed to be having some difficulties. In other words they had recurrent intense shouting matches. She did ninety five percent of the shouting. She could not get enough of pointing out her partner's failures and inadequacies. Week after week this went on. My customers would just stare at the wall in amazement. Finally one late Friday afternoon the boys stopped by my store on the way home from work to share a beer. We were having a great time when another argument erupted next door. This time it was particularly shrill. She really let him have it. Then he spoke. We all paused and listened. He said "I just want one thing from you". She screamed "And what's that?" In a faltering voice he responded "I just want you to… shut up!!!" Everyone in my store put down their beer, stood up and gave him a one minute round of applause complete with cheers and whistles. We never heard from them again.

When I first became a professional rare coin dealer I thought I knew a great deal about the hobby. In reality I knew next to nothing. I was as green and naïve as they come. When I first opened the door of my business, you could see the shark fins coming up my parking lot. They had come to test the new guy or "new meat" as they called it. The first thing I did was buy a counterfeit Rhode Island ship token (an early American copper) and some professionally cleaned Indian head cents (cleaning destroys any coin's value). I also sold some coins for thousands of dollars less than they were actually worth. Welcome to the neighborhood.

My rare coin business ran for three years. I have no regrets. I learned the equivalent of a college degree's worth of knowledge on how to deal with sharks, how to invest and how to spot bogus coins. Most importantly, I am keenly aware of how much I still don't know about this vast hobby.

Does this hobby have enough depth to hold an intelligent individual's interest? The books you need to properly educate yourself on the subject could easily fill one wall of a small library. In addition, the hobby can take you in any one of dozens of different directions. You can get involved in civil war tokens, hard times tokens (tokens dealing with the great depression of the 1830s), encased postage stamps, privately issued pioneer gold coins, rare branch mint gold coins, pattern coins (trial designs of coins that were never issued for general circulation. Some of the trial designs were unbelievably beautiful but too complicated to be struck on a massive scale), and colonial American copper coins (those coppers issued privately prior to the U.S mint opening in 1793). The early American copper collectors are true fanatics. These guys have really gone over the edge. Even good sex would take a back seat to examining a newly discovered group of New Jersey colonial coppers. Finally, you could just devote yourself to any one of the regular mint issues. Did you know that the United States at one time produced three cent pieces, two cent pieces, twenty cent pieces, half dimes and half cents as well as special silver dollar made for trade with the orient? There are also Indian peace medals which document every broken promise made to Native Americans. There are military medals, commemorative coins and the exquisite engraving of nineteenth century large paper currency. The list goes on and on. If you are bored with this hobby, it's your own fault.

Finally, there are more ways to get skinned alive investing in rare coins than you can count. Any area of collecting, whether it's guns, coins, watches, antiques etc. is full of real risk. Many coin dealers are former double glazing window salesmen and they are waiting for you. Part of the problem is that rare coins are truly rare. There aren't enough of them around to allow many dealers to make a living. So most of the coins at the coin shows are over graded, cleaned, whizzed, dipped, re-colored or otherwise toyed with. The dealer bought it for ten dollars and wants to sell it to you for five hundred dollars. Unless you know what you are doing you might be tempted to buy. Here are some hints on how to work your way around that problem.

First of all, go to as many coin shows as you can and don't buy anything. Instead just look at the coins. It takes a minimum of two years of full time looking at coins to develop the eye that you need to tell the good from the bad. There is no easy way to come by this knowledge. After all these years I still occasionally get fooled. If you do purchase coins in those first two years (it's hard to just look and not buy), whatever you do, keep your purchases at $50 or less. That way when you do make a mistake (and you will) it won't hurt too much.

Secondly, attach yourself to dealers who are interested in educating you. A truly smart dealer who wants your repeat business will use the education aspect of rare coins to form a dialogue with you. This will also help you gain access to other people who really love the hobby.

Every year the American Numismatic Association presents seminars on counterfeit coin detection. Attend those seminars. Travel great distances to get to them if you have to. If any object is worth money some clown will find a way to fake it. Many of the fakes are easy to spot. But some of the counterfeits even have the experts scratching their heads. Sometimes you just cannot tell if a coin is genuine. If any doubt exists in your mind, back away from the coin. Trust your instincts.

To give you an example of how sophisticated counterfeiters are, currently some ancient Roman gold coins are being produced using gold that actually came from ancient Rome (where the counterfeiters are obtaining the Roman gold I have no idea). So if you assay the gold in the fake, it comes out exactly right. The weight of the coin will also be perfect. One French counterfeiter made $20 United States gold coin fakes of such high quality that he actually signed them. He put a microscopic Greek Omega inside the eagle's claw on the coin's reverse.

What always fascinated me is that if some of these crooks put as much effort and talent into a regular job as they do making counterfeits, they could make a very good income, and not have to live with the fear of going to jail. But some people just cannot play a straight ball game.

Another important issue centers around coin grading. Grading a coin is crucial to establishing that coin's value. A numbered grading system of U.S coins has now gained widespread acceptance. The numbers run from one to seventy. A coin graded "1" has been crushed repeatedly by a steam roller. A coin graded "70" is perfect. As a general rule perfect coins don't exist before 1950. A coin is considered uncirculated once it reaches a grade of "60". Therefore that coin is called mint state (M.S.) 60. An M.S. 60 silver dollar can actually be an ugly coin even though it is technically uncirculated. Silver dollars are heavy coins. They came off a conveyor belt after being struck at the mint and landed on top of each other while being poured into a bucket. Then they were sewn into bags of a thousand coins each and loaded onto carts. Every time the bag gets tossed the coins collide with each other. The resulting abrasions on these coins are called "bag marks". During the nineteenth century silver dollars and twenty dollar gold pieces were used as collateral on bank loans across the United States; so the bags were loaded on and off trains and into bank vaults etc. etc. Thus most uncirculated coins don't have an attractive appearance. In addition, coins made out of copper, which is a very volatile metal, often developed black or green spots over time.

Furthermore, few people cared about coin collecting until the late 1800s. In economic hard times fifty cents was a lot of money. People couldn't afford to save their pocket change. Over time and exposure to elements the number of really attractive coins has been greatly reduced. In order to reflect the scarcity of better grade uncirculated coins the M.S. system gave a designation of M.S.63 to choice uncirculated specimens and M.S.65 to gem uncirculated coins. Coins that are graded M.S.66, 67, or 68 are superb gem uncirculated. These superior coins are very rare prior to 1878. But it gets even trickier. The finest recorded example of an early five dollar gold piece made at a branch mint may only grade about un-circulated (A.U.) 53. No uncirculated specimens are known to exist. So the finest known example may not even look that good. Population reports are compiled on each date and mint mark ("S" for San Francisco, "D" for Denver, "C" for Charlotte, "O" for New Orleans, "D" for Delongha (which went out of business prior to the opening of the Denver mint) "CC" for Carson City and no mint mark at all for coins minted in Philadelphia). So collectors usually know the top six coins in terms of condition for each date and mint. Looking at this from a non collector position one might ask "Well, who really cares?" But collectors do care. For instance an 1896 – "O" silver dollar in a nice circulated (very fine 30) condition is worth $25. In a slightly better (extremely fine 45) condition it is worth $30, which is not a huge jump. In M.S. 60 the same coin is worth $1075. In M.S. 65 it's worth $175,000 and M.S. 67 $575,000. That's quite a spread. So each point in uncirculated condition, depending on the coin, can result in a huge difference in value.

About forty years ago someone figured out that a dealer grading the same coin he was selling represented an inherent conflict of interest. Dealers were selling M.S. 60 coins as gem uncirculated. A lot of people fell into that trap, so the American Numismatic Association inaugurated an independent grading service. For a fee you could send a coin to the A.N.A. to be graded. A few weeks later your coin would be mailed back to you accompanied by a card. On that card was a photograph of the coin for identification purposes and an official grade. This was a stroke of genius and the A.N.A. was flooded with coins to be graded. Unfortunately, for whatever reason, the A.N.A. refused to pay the salaries necessary to get top notch graders. What were they thinking? So the grades returned on many of the cards turned out to be so unreliable that the cards were referred to as "toilet paper" by the numismatic trade. Talk about killing the goose that laid the golden egg. As a result, independent grading services emerged to meet the need for objective grading. There are currently roughly eight different grading services. Some of these services are pretty good, most are lousy. The bottom line is simple; there is no substitute for your own ability to grade a coin. That's why you should spend two years just looking at coins before making any significant purchase. Coin grading represents a consensus opinion. After looking at five hundred M.S. 63 coins, you should have a pretty good idea of what the consensus is for the M.S. 63 grade. If you don't proceed with this kind of caution, you will get badly burned.

As an additional note, once you do gain some confidence in your ability to evaluate a coin, buy the best coin you can afford. From an investment point of view that is the most fruitful long term strategy. Also, always buy coins that have a pleasing look to them. If you buy a coin with a serious problem (scratches, hair lines, detracting spots, rim dents, etc.) then when you eventually want to sell that coin you will have a problem. On the other hand a beautiful coin will always sell.

As a collector ages he or she often goes beyond the profit motive or the compulsive need to put round coins into round holes in coin albums. Early coins are just loaded with history. Coins outlast human beings and were often touched by many generations. Sometimes you can trace a coin to a specific historic event. A few years ago a Confederate half dollar was sold that was in the Confederate President Jefferson Davies' pocket when union troops arrested him. Early United States paper money often depicts cultural scenes in great detail from a bygone age. U.S colonial paper money often carried the message "To counterfeit is to die". No plea bargaining there. In fact Benjamin Franklin came up with a brilliant idea to deter counterfeiters. He impressed the image of a single leaf onto the colonial paper currency made at his printing shop. Since all leaves are different, the counterfeiter could not come up with an exact duplicate leaf image to place on their bogus script. Was Franklin not a clever man?

About a decade ago I attended a coin show in London. I asked a French dealer if he had any U.S. coins. He said in broken English "I have a Connecticut" meaning a colonial half penny made in Connecticut prior to 1793. I got excited. The coin handed me, however, was not a Connecticut copper, but was instead a true example of American Naïve

Art. It showed a primitive mountain range dotted with tiny pine trees completely out of scale with the mountains. The sun was rising behind the mountains and on the sun was a happy face. A plough was placed under the mountains as a tribute to agriculture and hard work. The legend contained the word "Vermonts". The coin was a Vermont landscape. There are less than six hundred known to exist and I've always wanted one. Vermont coins are almost always in poor condition, but this was a really nice example. I put on my best direct sales poker face, argued about the price for about three seconds and bought it.

In 1998 a fellow named Tony Carlotto, standing on the shoulders of researchers who went before him, published the definitive work on Vermont copper coinage. He went out of his way to bring the reader closer to early Vermont history. In 1785 when my coin was made, Vermont was a republic. If you travelled into the nether regions of this rugged country in winter, there was a real chance you weren't coming out. My coin was carried by pioneers who made that journey. By the way, how did that coin get to France? As Tony Carlotto says "If only the coins could talk". [1]

Years later in Hertfordshire, England, I purchased a bag full of early English coppers. Most of the coins were nothing special, but one coin fascinated me. Someone had taken the time to grind down a large English penny until it was a smooth blank on both sides. Then, with painstaking precision, he had used a pointed instrument to create via a series of dots an image of a man and a woman. The man had a pipe and a large hat, while the woman wore a dress with a bonnet. With such a crude instrument he could not create facial details, so his character's profiles were hidden by the hat and the bonnet. Despite its crude nature, the quality of the artwork was impressive. I kept wondering why, since this obviously took a lot of time, he had not used finer engraving tools.

The reverse of the coin contained a short love sonnet engraved with the same pointed instrument. The last line of this sonnet read "And whatever men may say of me, do not think of me unkind." This was followed by the date 1833. At the time I was a little short of cash, so like an idiot I sold the coin. Shortly afterwards I talked to a token expert who

---

[1] Carlotto, Tony, and The Colonial Coin Collectors Club, *The Copper Coins of Vermont.* Bookcrafters, Chelsea, MI. 1998, Page 6.

educated me concerning the origin of this token. The craftsman who made it did not have finer engraving instruments at his disposal because he was sitting in jail. He was probably using a pin or small knife. He was waiting to be deported from England to the penal colonies in Australia. Prior to departure he gave the coin to his lady. I've seen other cruder examples of these tokens since then. Sometimes the women followed their men to Australia. Sometimes the women never saw their lovers again.

The prisoner probably spent weeks making this piece. The woman in question either threw it away or kept it for the rest of her life. Either way, the coin I held gave me a genuine glimpse into their intimate history.

Chapter X

GOING POSTAL

England
24 April 2007

Another tragic outrage has just hit the front pages. I am referring to the mass execution at Virginia Tech. As often happens there was heroism. As always, there was a homicidal maniac. He even got his manifesto played on television. Did the television producers not realize that some wacko wannabies might be out there taking notes? What in the world makes these psychos think that the lives of others mean absolutely nothing? Unfortunately a true psychopath never seems able or willing to ask that question.

What bothers me even more is how desensitized society gets to the carnage. Every decade seems to present some new atrocity. Obviously human history is full of horrific events. But, over time, we like to think we are evolving in the right direction. Maybe not.

Almost immediately after a psycho's massacre, questions are raised about how to prevent the next catastrophe. Attention is always drawn to easy access to guns, and that is a very real issue. The English boast about their lack of gun violence when compared to their heavily armed American counterparts. Indeed, everyone in America does have the God given and constitutionally protected right to shoot everyone else.

But what the permissive British society doesn't tell you is that you are now more likely to be a victim of violent crime in London, Manchester and the West Midlands than in many major U.S. cities. It's hard to see the wonderful city of London in the same light as Detroit, but knife crime and gangs are out of control in both places.

The British press is fond of referring to the victim of a murderous assault as being "In the wrong place at the wrong time". Stop for a moment and take a good hard look at that phrase. The victim was in the *wrong* place at the *wrong* time. What is subtly implied is that the victim should have known better. After all, what was he doing in the "wrong place at the wrong time"? One can only conclude that the assault was at least partially the victim's fault. The British public comforts itself knowing that they would be careful not to be in the "wrong place at the wrong time".

Let's be clear about something. Unless you are standing directly in front of a tsunami, there is no such thing as "the wrong place at the wrong time". Instead, there are only the actions of really bad people. Therefore the efforts of individual citizens should focus more on stopping bad people from doing what they do. The fact that the average citizen concerns themselves with avoiding "the wrong place at the wrong time" betrays a sense of helplessness on the part of the public.

Returning to our discussion of almost random murders, how do we prevent the next attack by a sociopathic lunatic? Granted, stopping a major crime before it occurs is an extremely hard thing to do. But although everyone jumps on the pro or con gun bandwagon, few people seem to focus on the lunatic's psychopathic personality from a prevention point of view. We need to understand that even though the people who commit random murders may never have previously committed a major crime, their psychopathic behavior often leaves a trail. In the West Virginia killer's case it is obvious that the murderer had been making people nervous for some time. His whole focus was on violence. In all probability he got a real rush out of contemplating his future violent acts. So why wasn't he properly evaluated prior to the shooting spree?

(At this point I have to make an addendum. In August 2009, the Virginia Tech's murderer's medical records were made public by his family. Those records show that he was kept overnight in a psychiatric facility about a year prior to the massacre. A fellow student had overheard the patient in question threatening suicide. Inside the institution the patient convinced the medical practitioner that his comments about suicide were nothing more than a joke. This kind of denial on the part of psychiatric patients is common. Many of them don't want to end up on a locked ward with other psych patients. As a result, the patient will frequently downplay the seriousness of their intentions. Often psych patients will only tell the truth about their illness when that illness actually scares them, or when they are blatantly delusional. All of this shows that no method of psychiatric evaluation is foolproof).

Once in a great while in the emergency room I would deal with a child who scared me. I knew it was only a matter of time before he really hurt someone, but I couldn't prove it. School counselors can tell you stories that would curl your hair. We can all see it coming. But standard social wisdom dictates that you cannot incarcerate someone *before* they commit a crime. To do so would seem to fly in the face of the freedoms we enjoy in a democratic society. But agitation and aggression in a homicidal maniac will grow over time. Little offences by other people are seen as personal affronts. Finally the lunatic snaps and any offence is used as justification for ripping people apart with bullets. By that time intervention comes too late.

My basic argument is that there should be a way for concerned school counselors, social workers, teachers and family practitioners, etc. to insist that an individual must have a psychiatric evaluation. If, after a proper evaluation, lethal behavior is seen as a real possibility, then psychiatric inpatient hospitalization for, say, thirty days should be required. It is important to understand that you cannot cure these people. But sometimes the dangerous agitation can be defused and a slaughter prevented or at least delayed.

Obviously, if anyone is incarcerated prior to committing a crime their case must be reviewed on a regular basis. Knowing that he might be sued if the patient went out and killed someone, the attending psychiatrist might be too scared to authorize the patient's release. Instead, something this serious should be reviewed by an independent panel of three psychiatrists to whom the attending psychiatrist would make recommendations.

Any system that makes incarceration prior to a crime a real possibility must be carefully monitored to prevent abuse. Such a system is a scary thought. But the alternative is to do nothing. You can limit gun access as much as you want, but a highly motivated psychopath will eventually find whatever fire power they need.

I have to make another addendum. Any emergency room physician can involuntary commit a patient for a few days if the physician believes that the patient is a danger to themselves or others. Emergency physicians make these kinds of involuntary commitments frequently because there is so much psychopathology on the streets. But emergency commitments are usually a response to an acute event, such as a suicide attempt. What I am arguing for is a very careful broadening of these powers to include situations where non medical personnel believe real violence on the part of a patient is just a matter of time. Service personnel who make these recommendations in good faith would have to be immune from law suits. Parents are often in denial about how totally dangerous their little Johnny really is. Those same parents will often try legal intimidation tactics to protect their offspring.

I admit I am not entirely comfortable with these concepts. Some people who are just angry in the moment could be committed and labeled as dangerous. How do they get a job after that? But as one massacre follows another there is obviously a clear and present danger to society. It would be nice to get some of these people under psychiatric care *before* they pull the trigger. Toward that end we need some form of early screening for potentially violent behavior. As previously stated, we can all see it coming.

Chapter XI

ADVICE TO MEDICAL STUDENTS

As a medical student you will periodically find yourself thinking "It's not worth it." You might be right. No one ever said that medical training was going to be easy. But no one ever tells you what you will have to deal with once you become a physician. Try mountains of paperwork, and that's just the beginning. The bureaucrats who run health care have to look like they are doing something useful, otherwise they are out of a job. So one piece of paperwork after another will flow across your desk like they were poured out of the back of a dump truck. If you don't fill in the form, you don't get paid and/or your patient doesn't get that needed expensive M.R.I. scan. A friend of mine argued for twenty five minutes on the phone with a representative of an insurance company trying to get his patient a costly x-ray study. Finally the representative relented and said "O.K you can have that there test."

Can you imagine working for an insurance company and standing between patients and the medical care they need? I understand that the cost of medical care is sky rocketing. If you want to lower medical costs, cap medical malpractice awards given for "pain and suffering" at two hundred and fifty thousand dollars. A lot of expensive tests are ordered because the doctors know they can't be wrong about a diagnosis. One serious mistake in ten thousand patient visits can ruin you. More on that later.

The art and practice of medicine is a great experience. The only real problem is that you have to practice medicine on people. You have to trust me on this; the majority of human beings are flat out crazy. I am not talking about psychosis; I'm talking instead about complicated, tangled, maddening, frustrating neurosis. Numerous patients will invade your practice at least twice a week and just ventilate. After talking rapidly for about half an hour and at the same time giving you no clue about the nature of their medical concern, they feel better. Then they walk out until the next time. Taking time to listen to people is a real service. But if an Internist or General Practitioner falls more than thirty minutes behind in their daily schedule, they will never catch up with that day's work load. On a good day internists spend their lunchtime with a sandwich in one hand and writing emergency admission orders with the other. On a bad day the sandwich is missing, although most doctors would rather die than not eat. You have no idea how manic that day can be. I've stood in the Intensive Care Unit with one phone in my right ear, another phone in my left ear and a nurse talking to me all at the same time.

The staff lounge in most emergency rooms is packed with cookies and pastries. In our little community emergency room the members of the Ladies Auxiliary would regularly bake us cakes and pies. These elderly women were expert cooks. We worshipped them. Weight loss was impossible.

Leaving the subject of blessed food and returning to cursed patient neurosis, perhaps the most maddening thing is the patient's unwillingness to grapple with the true cause of their unhappiness. A woman who has had no affection from her husband during twenty five years of marriage will not talk about that; but she will return again and again with ill defined abdominal pain. Twenty five negative cat scans and thousands of dollars of expensive blood tests later, no pathology can be found. But the pain continues and she expects *you* the doctor, to find the cure. These patients have what I will call a dysfunctional algorithm for dealing with life's stressors. Many people just don't have the willingness to face the reality of their own lives.

In addition, a lot of folk thrive on the attention they get when they are seen by a doctor. This need for recognition can manifest itself with a wide range of clinical complaints. In one case the patient just wants a bit of your time. In another case the patient will undergo multiple and unnecessary surgeries rather than deal with their own issues. They are just plain nuts. Psychiatric referrals routinely don't help because the patient doesn't see their problem as psychiatric in origin.

Then there are the depressive and anxiety syndromes. Most of us will deal with our own depression and/or anxiety at some point in our lives. It's all part of being a member of the human race. Antidepressants are good drugs for organic depression. As stated before, however, most people are just plain crazy and there is no pill for that.

At this point, I am reminded of Ruby. Ruby was very elderly but not even vaguely senile and she looked twenty years younger than her stated age. She was intelligent, spry and self caring. But Ruby had a problem. She had what I will call a "dependency syndrome". Over time her anxiety levels would build and she would call for the ambulance. In just under three years Ruby called for the ambulance a hundred and fifty six times. Her story is absolutely fascinating, but because of medical confidentiality, I cannot say another word.

In rural towns, the ambulance is manned by unpaid voluntary Emergency Medical Technicians. The emphasis here is on the word "unpaid." These people are willing to get out of bed at two o'clock in the morning for no money just to bail your butt out of serious medical trouble if you should need them. The next day they had better hope that their bosses are understanding because they are half asleep on the job. But people with dependency syndromes don't seem to care how much stress they are placing on the local emergency medical services. They simply cannot step out of their own needs. So night after night the emergency medical providers have to leave their warm beds and answer calls that are simply unnecessary.

Dependency syndrome calls present another big problem. They present a direct danger to the local communities. While the ambulance is transporting a completely healthy patient to the hospital, another citizen of that same town might be having a heart attack. If someone does have a heart attack while Ruby is doing her song and dance, a second ambulance will respond from a neighboring village. But that will cause an eight to fifteen minute delay in the ambulance response time because the ambulance in the next town is further away. Eight to fifteen minutes doesn't sound like much, but with a heart attack or car accident, that delay can be critical. In addition, the crews from the next town might not be able to easily locate the address of the 911 call, simply because they don't live in the town where the call originated. Furthermore, if the ambulance is unsure how serious the call is, they will run with lights and sirens through intersections, and accidents will result no matter how cautious the ambulance crew tries to be. There is nothing worse than an ambulance hitting an oil slick on the road which results in the ambulance flipping over a guard rail and rolling down into a gulley. May you never see such a nightmare.

Although Ruby's case seems extreme, the personality traits that led to her behavior are actually very common. The United States contains hundreds of thousands of people with similar tendencies. They are everywhere.

Footnote No.1: Emergency Medical Technicians are routinely involved in administering life saving care and transport. Most of the time they deal with good people who are in difficult situations. But they often have to treat and transport the worst of humanity in what is often unbelievable circumstances. As previously stated, the EMTs work in small towns and do this night after night for no money. The soul of any town lies in its volunteer services.

Our small town came up with a really good idea. If you held on and donated twenty years of your life to the town's emergency ambulance services, you received a pension. The retired EMTs got about two hundred and thirty dollars a month. A lot of the people who volunteered all those years are not rich. During the day they were carpenters, stone masons, secretaries, teachers etc. Two hundred and thirty dollars might not sound like much, but that money could buy a retired person a month's worth of medication, or a month's worth of gas, or a back seat full of groceries. When you're old, that's no small deal.

Besides the value of the money in old age, it's also a very proper "thank you" for all those years of sleepless nights. It's a nice touch after twenty years of your psychos for nothing and your drunks for free. I recommend that every town come up with a similar policy. In addition to showing gratitude, that pension will act to keep the more experienced staff on active duty until they reach twenty years of service.

Assuming that you still want to be a doctor, let's focus on ways to survive medical training. The first thing to realize is that while in medical school it is very easy to sink your own ship. At some point in your training, endurance becomes more important than intelligence. There are a lot of very mentally able people who could never become doctors. The stress of the training alone would crush them.

Sinking your own ship begins when you start to torture yourself with doubts about your own ability. Every medical student goes through this. "Do I really want to be a doctor?" "Is anything worth what I am going through?" "I'm just plain homesick." "I could never accomplish what they are asking of me." These doubts can lead to a spiraling depression that is difficult to reverse. Here are some hints on how to cope with medical training:

1. Don't look at the big picture. At the beginning of medical school, looking at all that lies before you is like standing at the bottom of Mount Everest with a pair of climbing shoes, a pick and a short rope. Focus only on the next exam or the next shift, etc., and do what you have to do to get ready for that. One step at a time.

2. Keep balance in your life. If you're going to work hard, play hard. Studying hours and hours a day is not a normal or natural existence. Physical exercise is the key to survival. You won't sleep well without it, and a good night's sleep is crucial to getting ready for the next day's challenges. Jogging works for many people. My salvation was basketball. I played very little basketball as a child, so when I started playing in medical school I was terrible. But the Brooklyn boys gave me some hints and soon I was living for the game after the day's classes were over. I was a member of a team called "White Man's Disease" because none of us could jump.

3 Frequent sex is a good idea. Nothing clears an academically overloaded mind like a solid orgasm.

4. As a rule, never lose touch with life. The students in our medical school class who became the best doctors were usually not the ones with the highest test scores. The best doctors were the ones who had lives prior to going to medical school. Those life experiences allowed them to connect to their patients. They had been there and done that. In essence, never stop being human.

5. Be good to yourself. You are at least as important as any of your patients. Find a way to build treats into each day (but watch out for food overload). Give yourself something that will make you smile when the day's work is done.

6. In all but the most extreme circumstances, take one day completely off a week. Just put the books down and leave the campus. A little fresh air is crucial. Your brain needs time to reset itself.

7. Don't panic. So you just got a "C" in histology. So what? That "C"

means you can forget about histology and move on. You just removed one more hurdle that stands between you and graduation. For many students a "C" in pre-med was a prelude to contemplating suicide. More than a few "C" grades meant you would never get into medical school. But medical school is different than college. We used to comfort ourselves with the equation "C = M.D." Just get through the day. On the other hand, put a lot of effort into courses like physiology and pathology which explain how disease actually works in the human body. That knowledge you cannot do without.

8. Once the major exams are over, party like an animal. Don't die in a drunken car accident and don't fall off a tall building. In fact, don't do any activity from which you cannot fully recover. Anything else is acceptable. If a quiet movie does it for you, that's fine. But whatever you do, remember why you are alive.

Footnote No.2: After two years of grueling academic work and impossible international exams, we were finally set loose on real patients in a supervised setting. At last, a dose of reality. We were starting our first clinical rotation in a local Caribbean hospital. Wearing virginal white coats and brand new cheap stethoscopes, we boarded the mini bus that would take us to that small hospital.

The foundation of clinical training is the patient history and physical exam. Knowing how to do that properly takes years of experience. As medical students, we knew we had to ask at least three thousand questions of every patient. A few of those questions concerned bowel movements. It had been repeatedly drummed into our brains that we had to ask each patient about the character of their stools, even if their main complaint was a persistent cough. A change in the size or character of stools could indicate bowel cancer. Bloody stools could again suggest cancer, any number of infections, or autoimmune bowel disease such as Chrone's disease or colitis. In addition, black tarry stools could be digested blood oozing from a dangerous bleeding ulcer high up in the G.I. tract.

Armed with this knowledge, my friend Joe from Newark sat down with his first island native patient. Joe asked his patient "What do your stools look like?" The patient responded "I don't know, man." Joe tried again "Are your stools black or bloody?" Again the patient replied "I don't know, man." Once again Joe asked "Have your stools changed in size or character?" For the third time the patient responded "I don't know, man." Finally Joe leaned back in his chair and asked "Well, why don't you know?" The patient stared at Joe and said "It's dark down the hole, man!" It was a classical example of New Jersey meeting the Caribbean.

Chapter XII

BEQUIA

Some of my fondest memories are of the little Caribbean island called Bequia. Bequia sits at the top of the Grenadine chain between St Vincent and Grenada. Because of its physical isolation, it was unspoilt when I was there some twenty five years ago.

Bequia is separated from the larger island of St Vincent by an ocean trench thousands of feet deep and nine miles wide. The only access to Bequia was by sail boat, the occasional private sea plane, or the Bequia ferry. The Bequia ferry is a tramp steamer full of natives, coconuts, bananas and life. Several times a week this condensed microcosm of Caribbean society would plough the waves over to Bequia. Babies were born on that boat. Goats would bleat, indicating their concern over their unsure future. On a sunny day it was a voyage to pure freedom.

Our medical courses were taught in intense two week blocks. At the end of those two weeks we took a do or die written exam. After that we had the weekend off before the next two week cycle began. The ink on our test papers wasn't even dry before we were scrambling onto the local Rasta minivan to take us to the Bequia ferry. Small speakers on the minivan would blast us with Reggae music as we careened down the mountain road. The bus drivers were often stoned, but no one seemed to care. We all had the essentials in our book bags; clean socks and underwear, a bathing suit and cold beer. Life began. The ferry trip itself was a healthy transition. The clean wind and salt spray blew all the academic dust from our brains. We kicked back. While sipping our beers we watched tourists vomit over the side of the boat. Eventually the ferry chugged its way into a horseshoe shaped lagoon. A peaceful scene was spread out before us. There's one main street on Bequia which runs only as far as the waterline beside the lagoon. There are just a handful of tourist shops and restaurants. With a little extra cash you can eat a fresh steamed lobster while listening to the waves lap against the shore. Not bad.

But unfortunately there was never any extra money for us students. We were chronically short of cash, so we shared the cheapest hotel room we could find. This meant, among other things, that the electrical generator for the hotel would be turned off from 9.00 pm until the next morning. Thus, after 9.00 pm there was no shower, no running water in the sink and only one flush left in the toilet. If you drank too much in the bar that night you had a problem. Since there were four of us in one small room, we all had a problem.

Nursing a hangover, we often awoke to the sweet sounds of a goat and a rooster slugging it out in the back yard. We regrouped for breakfast and afterward took a long cliff side walk to the beach. Each of the island's two main beaches are composed of gleaming white sand about twenty feet wide and a hundred yards long. The sand slides gracefully into calm turquoise blue waters. About a hundred feet off shore, a floating platform laid anchored to the bottom of the lagoon. Having made the easy swim to the platform, you could gently float on the waves. In addition, there were two hammocks strung between palm trees that sat on the back of one of the beaches. The bar was a dozen feet away from the hammocks. The sky was awash with shades of blue. An occasional puffy white cloud would slide by in the breeze. I don't know how we coped.

Nothing in the Caribbean runs on a strict schedule. You'll hemorrhage if you bring your New York state of mind down here. The natives do what feels right at the moment. The intense mid day sun slows everything down. You just have to go with the flow.

One evening John, Roz and I were sitting at a waterside café when John said "Sam, is that the Bequia ferry leaving port?" I swung around in my chair. It could only be the Bequia ferry since it was ten times larger than anything else in the harbor. "Oops, it was supposed to leave tomorrow morning!" We were marooned on Bequia. Did we have enough money for one more night? We all threw our remaining E.C. (Eastern Caribbean currency) onto the center of the table. We had just enough money to make it happen. "Bartender, one more round." Why argue with fate?

132

We often sat in a bar at sunset and watched for the "green flash." Personally, I don't think this exists. But people all over the islands pause as the sun slowly descends through the pink and green pastels of the Caribbean sunset. The instant the sun disappears below the water, there is supposed to be a green flash. Bars everywhere are at a standstill at that moment. Key West has a green flash party every evening. I have given this natural phenomenon my intense concentration night after night. All I am ever able to see when the sun disappears is that black dot that appears in your line of sight just after you have stopped looking at the sun. I am currently applying for grant money for further research on this topic.

Everyone who has been in the Caribbean more than sixty days has an interesting story to tell. Just have a friendly smile and a warm hello and you'll get to meet some of these remarkable people. One young couple I met had Caribbean sightseeing down to a fine art. For a few E.C. they would hop a local banana boat. You can't get excited about where that boat is going or when it will get there. You just ride the waves knowing that the boat's crew knows every ocean current and wind pattern. You will arrive somewhere at sometime. After saying farewell to the crew, Doug and Janet would get a bite to eat and then buy a large bottle of rum and a lot of little paper cups. In the early 1980s a Caribbean island's monthly social security payment to the elderly didn't amount to much. The money was just adequate to buy enough rum to make you forget about how poor you were. Night after night the old island men would sit on rickety chairs in front of ancient wooden tables and play endless games of dominoes. They were very serious about their game. The decisive domino would start its downward journey toward the table from high above the old man's head. It would then be slammed onto the table with a thunderous finality. Don't ever bet against these guys.

The nightly domino ritual usually occurred in the market place or town square. Doug and Janet would walk up to the natives and strike up a friendly conversation. Pretty soon the paper cups and rum were being distributed. After a few hours of laughs and stories, our couple knew everything worth knowing about that particular island. They knew what to see, where to go and just as important where not to go. This approach is pure genius. You make friends and avoid pitfalls. In addition, if you can leave the unfortunately typical condescending American and British attitude behind, you will receive a gift. You will see the true Caribbean through the eyes of people that have lived there their whole lives. In contrast, the tourist hotels will put up fancy lights, throw lavish parties, blare loud music and distribute pool side bingo cards. All of this is just a smoke screen that will blind you to the wonderful grounding experience that awaits you on these islands.

One night, again in a bar (no, I'm not an alcoholic) I met a middle aged lady from Norway. During our conversation I learned how to raise sheep above the Arctic Circle. That's where her daughter and son-in-law have a farm. Apparently the key is to get the new born lamb out of the gestational sack and dry it off before it freezes to death.

Several years prior to our bar side meeting, this lady had received a diagnosis of terminal cancer. She quit her job, sold the house and divorced the bastard. Then she got a few friends together, bought a sailboat and spent two years sailing around the world. When the voyage was finished she returned to see her doctor. After a complete workup, the doctor told her that her cancer had disappeared. Now she had to deal with an unexpected normal life span. She got a job as a school bus driver. But every year she rounds up her friends, rents a sail boat and spends a few weeks sailing the Caribbean waters. Why leave that healing experience behind?

On a completely different note, Joe and I were eating a quiet dinner at a bay side restaurant on Bequia. Unexpectedly, two young German girls sat down at our table. They were of course beautiful. We had met them on the beach earlier in the day and passed a pleasant afternoon between their broken English and my pathetic ten words of German. (They let me through my two years of college German with the tacit understanding that I would never try again). But now the girls had a dilemma. They were running very short of money and had nowhere to spend the night. Would we mind if they stayed in our room? Joe and I looked at each other. We had been under constant academic pressure. We had not seen an eligible woman for months. Could it be that our ship had finally come in? I debated the ethics of the situation for a greater part of a second and said "O.K."

Back in the room, the girls stripped down to almost nothing and curled up on two blankets on the floor. I turned out the light. The generator ceased functioning. It was very quiet. Joe turned to me and said "Sam, I can't sleep". There was desperation in his voice. I tried to strike up a conversation with the girls, but got little response. They really just wanted a dry roof over their heads. Joe and I stared holes in the ceiling for about another hour. Then Joe turned to me and uttered the line that will stay tattooed in my brain for the rest of my life. He said, "Sam, no jury in the world would convict us". I told him to go to sleep.

The night passed in an uneventful manner. In the morning we shared a casual breakfast with the girls. Afterwards they smiled at us and were on their way. Sigh!

Dave was a medical student who should have been a Green Beret officer. He, Mongo and I were sitting at another waterside establishment in Bequia. Rum is cheap in the Caribbean so the native bar tender was playing games seeing how wasted he could get the medical students. I knew I would be holding Dave's head over the toilet that night. But then fate played a little trick. Dave slid over to me at the bar and said "Sam, you have to hear this story"! I looked up and saw a young lady at the end of the bar with tears in her eyes. She was simply gorgeous; and a true damsel in distress. God knows two drunken medical students would do anything to help. Her story is as follows: Our heroin had herself been a medical student in Denmark. She started a relationship at that time with a guy who talked her into quitting medical school. At roughly the same time, a local rich businessman had constructed a sail boat. But this was not just any sailboat. It was built in the style of a nineteenth century Danish sailing vessel. There were none of those particular sail boats left to copy, so he had to have the sixty-footer hand crafted from some blue prints he found in a library. No expense was spared. For example, the hull was lined with copper to prevent worm rot. He then hired our heroin and her lover to sail his creation to New Zealand (I don't know why). But the duty required to admit this one of a kind craft into New Zealand turned out to be prohibitively expensive. So the owner told them to sail to the Caribbean (just a hop and a skip across the Pacific Ocean) and try to make some money running a chartered yacht service. About a month prior to our encounter in Bequia, the man (call him Franz and her Chris) developed left ear pain. He had some outdated tetracycline on board and he took that without much relief. Finally he found some amoxicillin over the counter in a port pharmacy, and that seemed to do the trick. His ear pain resolved. About a month later he started to lose weight. Nausea and vomiting began. She knew enough to keep him hydrated, but he was capable of holding down no more than a boiled egg a day. Eventually he got too weak to stand. The immediate problem centered around the fact that the sail boat was so large that she couldn't sail it by herself. Anchored in Bequia harbor, they were truly stuck. In the third world it is possible to get quickly into deep trouble with no way out.

Dave and I decided that the next reasonable step would be to examine Franz. So, near midnight, Chris took us back to the mother ship in a small inflatable dingy. In the dark bow of the ship we found Franz. He was tall, late forties and cachectic to the point that he looked like a survivor from a concentration camp. After talking to and examining him I concluded that he had an intra abdominal carcinoma causing gastric outlet obstruction. He vomited soon after eating almost anything. The next morning Dave was strong enough to get Franz up the gang plank to the Bequia ferry. Chris and I followed. Once back at St Vincent, we consulted a very bright young British physician who was volunteering at the St Vincent hospital. Initially he agreed with my diagnosis and Franz was admitted. The St Vincent hospital does good work, but they didn't have the high tech equipment needed to work up a complicated patient like Franz. But much to our surprise, his preliminary blood work and x-rays all came back normal. The young British physician did what any good clinician would do in this situation. He sat down with the patient, hit the text books hard and started the work up all over again. He came up with a brilliant diagnosis. It seems that outdated tetracycline can cause something called a Fanconi syndrome. This results in renal damage which allows massive amounts of protein to leak out into the urine. The loss of protein results in severe fatigue and weight loss. Nausea and vomiting soon follow. The good news is that if you can survive the starvation, the symptoms abate after four to six weeks. They kept him hydrated with I.V. fluids in the hospital, put him on a high calorie liquid diet and soon Franz's strength began to return.

Dave had an off campus apartment and during the hospitalization Chris spent time there. To show you how different some people's lifestyles are, it was Chris' first night on dry land in seven years.

Franz made a full recovery. A few weeks after discharge from the hospital, Dave waved goodbye as they sailed into the sunset.

As fate would have it, I found a question on outdated tetracycline on every one of my subsequent medical board exams. In medicine you are only as good as what you have seen clinically. Medical students have to study very intensely about various disease states. However, the dry medical information leaks slowly out of your brain like water out of a sieve. But once you have seen a patient with a specific illness and etched their face into your mind, you will never forget what you have learned. Chris and Franz's faces are still with me, along with the grace and charm of an island called Bequia.

Chapter XIII

ADVICE TO MEDICAL RESIDENTS

Once you graduate from Medical School, you are looking down both barrels of a medical or surgical residency. But the survival tactics we just discussed apply here as well. Again, just take one day at a time.

I remember one nice fellow who was a patient in our Coronary Care Unit. He had just opened his own business a few months prior to having his first heart attack at the age of forty one. He felt under tremendous pressure to make his business work and was putting in seventy hours a week toward that end. Obviously he had a genetic predisposition to early heart attacks, but the stress of his current life had proved unbearable. So we talked about ways to reduce his stress and delegate some of his obligations. The bottom line was that a seventy hour work week wasn't going to fly in a forty one year old. As I walked away, I realised that I was forty one years old and working eighty to a hundred and ten hours a week as a medical intern. I felt momentary palpitations. A diet Coke with ice and lemon made it all better.

Internship at age forty one proved to be an interesting way to spend a year. I had a salt and pepper beard, so patients assumed I was in charge. As an intern you are truly dangerous. You are a physician, can prescribe medications and know very little. The I.C.U. and C.C.U. nurses and respiratory therapists watched us very closely, thank God.

Our residency program was a good one. Our mentors were also our friends which made a tremendous positive difference in our day to day routine. We were never belittled and our standard of care was high. Poor people travelled from more than a hundred miles away to be on our service. When the medical care is good, word quickly gets around among poor folk.

Having survived medical residency, I can only think of a few general pieces of advice to give those who are on that residency treadmill. First, repeat after me; "If you don't look, you don't find." The foundation of good medical care really is the patient's history and physical. You have to be truly anal and absolutely dedicated to uncovering the truth. Take the tough complicated patient as a personal challenge. The initial patient's work up can be difficult. Some patients are graduates of the "St Theresa School for the Vague". They are literally incapable of giving you a straight answer to any simple medical question. They just cannot move from point "A" to point "B" in their thinking. Their brains don't work that way. It's easier to squeeze water out of a rock than to get useful medical information out of them. Sometimes it helps to just walk away from these patients and try again later, time permitting. The patients can then think about your questions and that might help a bit.

A lot of hospitals use printed forms for their history and physicals. It saves time and is in theory a more complete way of doing things. In the very small space provided for you to write the results of your exam you might enter a scribbled "W.N.L.", which means the result of that section of your physical exam was "within normal limits". One medical student explained to me that "W.N.L." really means "We never looked."

Never lie to your patients or your mentors. Once the bond of trust is broken, you can never get it back. This is particularly true when you are working with psychotics who are paranoid. A psychotic may not be able to tell which of the voices they are listening to are real, but they can sniff out a lie in a heartbeat.

One scary story circulated while we were in our training. On a surgical ward round the residents gathered around the patient's bed along with the Chief of Surgery. The Chief asked the intern who had done the patient's admission history and physical if the patient had adequate dorsalis pedis pulses (pulses in the top of the feet). The intern responded "Yes sir, he does." The Chief then ripped back the sheet covering the patient's body. The patient had previously received bilateral below the knee amputations. In other words, he had no feet. It's difficult for an intern to recover credibility after a situation like that.

Looking ahead to graduation, whatever you do, do not practice in a state where "pain and suffering" awards have not been capped at $250,000. You cannot afford malpractice insurance that will cover an almost unlimited award given by a jury that has no concept of what medical practice is all about. The jury often treats the malpractice award as a lottery win for the patient. They don't understand that there is no such thing as a free lunch. The insurance companies will simply jack up the malpractice premiums to cover the unreasonable award. This has the effect of putting adequate insurance out of reach of both hospitals and individual practitioners. This is not a futuristic concern. Currently, no emergency room physician group can afford coverage of more than one million dollars per physician. This is totally inadequate. Multimillion dollar "pain and suffering" awards are common. I know of one award that went for thirty million dollars. (It's important to understand that "pain and suffering" awards are in addition to whatever it costs to pay for the patient's continuing care). To make matters worse, I talked to one hospital risk manager who told me that in Florida, every other doctor is sued every other year. We are talking about the impending paralysis of the health care industry.

About the time I retired, OB-GYN physicians were leaving my home state like the place was on fire. The statute of limitations on malpractice suits is three years from the *time of discovery of the fault*. Learning disabilities in children are very common. Difficult or prolonged childbirths are also very common, and, once in a while, unpredictable. If a malpractice lawyer can find a *possible* connection between the learning disability and the difficult delivery which, in the best of all possible worlds, *might* have been prevented, you are looking at a lifelong disability award. Little Johnny did not get into Harvard, and it's your fault.

Despite a march on the capital attended by one third of the state's physicians, the "pain and suffering" award problem was not corrected. The legislators were in the pockets of the trial lawyers, and nothing could be done.

No matter how good your clinical skills may be, the baseball will eventually go between your legs. At that point, all you can hope for is that the patient or the family will be understanding.

If you work in an environment where you know your medical malpractice insurance is inadequate, then every patient presents a potential for financial ruin. You will find yourself asking, "Is this the patient who will cause me to lose everything I own?" You could lose your house and the kid's college fund, which you spent years putting together. Everything that is not in an irrevocable trust is potentially up for grabs. Once a lawsuit is initiated, it is illegal to move money to a protected place. Putting the house in your spouse's name doesn't work either. Even if you are just starting out and have nothing, the plaintiff's lawyers can attach your future pay checks. There is no escape from the hounds of hell. You also have to worry about the lawsuit's outcome for five years before the case goes to court. It is unreasonable to ask medical practitioners to work under this kind of pressure.

The best way to prevent lawsuits is to be a good communicator. If you walk into the patient's room with a warm smile and a genuine interest in the patient's medical problem, things will go well 98% of the time. But if you walk in with a fatigue driven frown and an attitude that lets the patient know that he is the only thing between you and lunch, then an adversarial doctor – patient relationship begins. Nothing good will come out of that. If you are dog tired, explain to the patient that you had a rough night. Most people will understand. If things medically do go belly up, talk to the people involved. I know of one ugly lawsuit that came as a result of the physician simply leaving the hospital after the patient died. The family later told me that they would not have sued if someone had just said "I'm sorry." and explained what had happened to the patient.

Turning the page to another issue, in the words of one of my colleagues, doctor G.K., "The best medicine is performed when everyone involved has had an egoectomy." Those words should be up in lights in every hospital. If you are a doctor and you think everyone outside of you is an idiot, the patient will pay a terrible price. If you intimidate interns, nurses and paramedics, they will keep their mouths shut in terms of useful suggestions. They are afraid of being made to look foolish in public. They are also quietly waiting for the egotistical doctor to fall flat on his face, which eventually he will do. But while everyone keeps their mouths shut, good suggestions about the patient's care are not being made. The king indeed walks around without any clothes, but the patient lies in the shadow of his arrogance.

While working, I always tried to involve nurses and paramedics in the medical decision making process. Four experienced minds working on a tough patient problem are always better than one. In the final analysis, you just have to ask yourself "What matters most, the patient's well being or my ego?"

One night towards the end of my residency, I was on call for the medical wards. It was midnight and I walked around to each nurse's station asking if they had any patients with problems prior to my trying to catch a few hours sleep. While I was walking down one ward, I noticed the television on in a room that contained no patients. Out of curiosity I entered the room. One of the night shift janitorial staff had turned on the T.V. She was leaning against the mop which she had placed in a bucket full of soapy water. She was in her fifties, had thick, black shoulder length hair with a few strands of grey scattered throughout. Her face was thin and chiseled by years of hard work. She looked at the T.V. through Coke bottle glasses. I turned my attention to the T.V. screen bolted onto the wall. She was watching the latest T.V. evangelist to be caught with a prostitute. I remember what the prostitute had told the newspapers after all was said and done. Referring to the evangelist, she said "He's kind of strange. I wouldn't want him around my kids." I live for moments like this.

On the T.V., the evangelist had tears running down his face. He was begging his flock to forgive him. But the object of my interest was the cleaning lady. She was watching the evangelist with great intensity. I thought to myself "We are all sheep. How could people be so easily led by such an obvious con artist?" She picked up the mop and bucket and exited the room. On her way out she turned to me and said "Cries good for money, don't he?" My faith in humanity was instantly restored.

It's one small step for mankind but one huge leap for you when your residency is completed. A golden opportunity now awaits you. I'm not talking about being a physician and reversing severe illnesses, or becoming a pillar of your local community. I'm talking instead about your ability to earn *real money*! *Yes*!!! After eight years of college and medical school followed by three to six years of gut wrenching residency, poverty is about to end. The promised land is in sight! Your debts and student loans total well over two hundred and fifty thousand dollars. Your car exhaust is held up by a coat hanger which is duck taped in place. You worked eighty hours a week for approximately the same wage as a doorman. Your clothes are five years old. Your shoes had to be resoled due to all the time you spent on your feet. The edges of all your credit cards are smoking. But you just opened your own medical practice and signed a low six figure guaranteed income contract with the local hospital. This will support you for three years until your patient base grows to a self sustaining level. Poverty has ended. You are now making four times as much money as you have ever made in your life.

It's time to celebrate. You stride to your local BMW dealership and buy that M3 convertible that you've been lusting after all these years. Golfing membership at the local club seems like a requirement. You leave the roaches in your current apartment behind and buy the big house on the hill. Six months later, you purchase a condo on the Outer Banks of North Carolina. Then you buy your sweet wife a one carat markee cut diamond ring. This, by the way, is your second wife. Your first wife was left all alone during your residency with two screaming colicky brats. Even when you came home, you were too tired to talk to her; so she developed panic attacks followed by a huge craving for Valium. As a result of your absence, she began to look forward to the daily delivery by that fine young mail man. He was just out of rehab for benzodiazepam dependence, so he formed an instant bond with your wife. Finally they ran off together along with one of your prescription pads. Your folks are now raising the kids. Thank god for grandparents.

As the ship of your marriage began to sink, that cute little I.C.U. nurse proved to be irresistible. After all, by midnight in the I.C.U., everyone is in their pajamas (scrubs). She was just coming off an abusive relationship with a biker and fell into your sympathetic arms. She's now pregnant with your first child together. Fortunately she seems to be able to deal with the pregnancy and looking after her two other kids from a previous marriage. If you can deal with the I.C.U., you can deal with anything. Things are looking up.

Your failed first marriage is now behind you, except for the fact that your oldest boy likes to start fires. He seems to be angry about something. He ends up in psychotherapy twice a week.

So, you see a few patients a day in your brand new practice and pick up your big pay check every two weeks. What a relief. Could this be what normal life is really all about?

But then a disturbing trend starts to occur. Bills start to fill your mailbox. The powers that be want all of that student loan money back with interest. You now have two mortgages along with car payments. Playing golf is never free. Let us not forget those divorce lawyer payments, plus your boy's psychotherapy costs about one hundred dollars an hour. Your second wife is not working due to her pregnancy, and her kids need supporting. You look hard at your big pay check and come to a stunning realization. It's not enough money. Could this be possible? Now what do you do? It will be years before your practice generates greater income. There is only one possible solution. You close your practice at 5.00 pm and work the 6.00 pm to 2.00 am shift in the local emergency room two nights a week and every other Saturday and Sunday. The extra money helps a lot.

Time goes by and fatigue starts to set in. A horrible feeling begins to emerge. You hate the practice of medicine. You start to feel trapped. You look at your step daughter's hamster running nonstop inside the wheel in its cage. You realize that you and that hamster have a lot in common.

One night you get home from the E.R. at 2.45 am. You know you have to be at the hospital for ward rounds at 7.30 am, but you can't sleep. The E.R. that night was beyond a disaster. Three teenagers at a rave came in seriously ill on an overdose of God knows what. One of them was in a coma and had to be placed on a ventilator. The kid's parents went crazy and demanded to know who had slipped drugs to their unsuspecting beloved child. A friend of the kid told one of the nurses that the child on the ventilator had done so many drugs in the past that if she did end up with brain damage, it would be impossible to know when it happened.

Then a mother and her live-in boyfriend ran into the emergency room carrying a shaken baby. The boyfriend looked very uncomfortable. The cops were called.

Shortly afterwards two teenage girls who had been at the same rave showed up complaining that they had been raped, they think. Part of the problem with date rape drugs is that the drugs cause an amnesia. A proper rape evaluation takes at least an hour per patient. If the train of evidence is not documented at any point in the rape evaluation, some scum bag lawyer will get the perpetrator off on a technicality. The nurse that is trained to do these evaluations is on vacation, so you had to stumble your way through it. The girls, still feeling the effects of the drug and lots of alcohol, weren't even rational. Doing a pelvic exam on a hysterical patient is impossible. Sedating the girls prior to doing a pelvic exam is out of the question. You don't know how your sedating medication is going to interact with whatever substances of abuse they took at the rave. Furthermore, sedating a minor in a non life threatening situation without parental consent is illegal and the single mother is nowhere to be found. So, you did pregnancy tests on both girls and one of those tests came back positive. Vaginal smears and blood work were sent to the lab to test for sexually transmitted diseases. The non pregnant girl was sixteen years old. After a few hours she did sober up enough for you to complete a pelvic exam. During that exam you noted precancerous cervical erosion from human papilloma virus. She obviously has been sexually active for years. Several serious sexually transmitted diseases have a long incubation period. Thus a blood test for those diseases (like H.I.V. and hepatitis B and hepatitis C) will need to be drawn repeatedly over the next six months. Somehow you know the girl will not keep her follow up clinic appointments.

But the coup de gras was a van ramming into a tree at 11:00 pm. All five passengers were unbelted. The two adults, a man and a woman, were killed instantly. While pronouncing them dead, you could smell alcohol on both corpses. One of the three children is in neuro surgery with a severe intracranial bleed and probably will not survive. Another little girl got away with just a broken arm. She keeps asking "Where's Daddy?" As it turns out, the deceased adult female was not the little girl's mother. The third child cannot feel anything from the waist down. He was transferred to the regional spinal unit. Social services, already stretched with the rape cases, could not find any indication of a permanent address. They were probably transients. The license plate on the van was from Oklahoma. A call was placed to a telephone number found in the man's wallet. It turned out to be his mother. On hearing the bad news she screamed "I can't handle this!" and slammed the phone down on the receiver. That was probably followed by a bolus of her "nerve pills" and a Seagram's chaser. So who's going to take care of the kids? Once again social services has a huge job in front of them.

Adding contour to the E.R.'s chaos were the three patients who were blind drunk. One of them turned violent and had to be gang tackled by the security forces. You treated the nurse he punched. The violent drunk's best buddy got upset by all of this and vomited on the nursing station desk, which was covered with patients' charts. The third drunk walked into a room where the local bank vice president was having his first heart attack. The drunk quietly pissed into one corner of the room. The patient's chest pain got worse as a result, but his blood pressure and pulse fortunately remained stable. The bank vice president's wife was even less impressed since her new sable coat was lying on a chair in that same corner.

Two additional men were brought in from a moderately severe car wreck. They did not seem to be seriously hurt, but precautionary x-rays were done. While waiting for the x-ray results, one of the men was caught stealing money from a purse belonging to a little old lady patient who was sleeping on a stretcher. On being frisked by security, both men had several books from the emergency room medical library under their belts. Each book had to do with the toxic effects of drugs. It's nice to keep up to date in an ever changing market.

As you were exiting the emergency room at 2.15 am, you walked by the examination room nearest the E.R. entrance. Inside that room was a lady with a bad cough. Her care had been delayed for hours due to the van accident and the rape cases. She was a welfare patient. Tax dollars have paid for her upkeep most of her life. The same is true of her three kids. As you walk by, she was screaming at the top of her lungs "I know my *rights!*" She knew that by disrupting the entire emergency room she would receive the attention she wanted. She was well acquainted with the system.

At 3:00 am you quietly slip into bed. You are beyond exhaustion. As a result of the evening's events you lie in bed and vibrate in place. You are a sponge filled with your own adrenalin. Making matters worse is the knowledge that you only have a few hours before the starting gun goes off for the next day's challenges. You try watching some stupid late night television, but that doesn't work. You pour yourself a double scotch. It's a twenty year old single malt. You can now afford the best stuff. It tastes so good. You pour another double. At last sleep becomes possible. At last.

As the months go by, you find yourself more and more exhausted by the extra emergency room shifts. Your second wife gave birth to a healthy baby boy, but like your first two kids, he cries a lot. Sleep becomes disturbed for the next six months. The scotch seems to be the only reliable way to let it all go.

Finally one morning after arriving at the hospital for ward rounds, the charge nurse smells alcohol on your breath. She blows the whistle, as she must. Now the ugly dragon called The Drug Enforcement Administration (D.E.A.) awakens. Your prescriptive powers are suspended. Your practice comes to a grinding halt. Whether you are truly an alcoholic or not, you must submit yourself to a thirty day in-patient drug and alcohol rehabilitation program. Somehow the local paper gets wind of your story. Questions start to be asked about some of your patients who had bad medical outcomes. "Was our doctor drunk when he treated Granddad?" was one headline you noticed when you filled up your car at the gas station. The hospital's risk manager suggests that you get legal counsel. Your reputation takes a huge hit.

After leaving rehab you get limited prescriptive powers back. But your narcotic prescriptions have to be checked and co-signed by another physician for the next six months. How do you do that in a single handed private practice? You submit to the required monthly drug and alcohol blood tests. Of course your creditors are very understanding during this period.

Any way you look at it, there are many mechanical ambushes awaiting young doctors in the modern medical world. I knew a fine physician who had five good kids and a strong wife. He worked very hard and gave all the kids a college education. But recently he confided to another friend of mine that his hard work had resulted in his being absent from most of his childrens' early years. What a mistake. He can never get that time back. If you are going to immerse yourself in your work, force yourself to schedule time in advance to immerse yourself in your family. They need you. No excuses. You don't want your kids starting fires.

If you are a female physician, do not have babies during your residency. I have seen good strong women collapse under that strain. If you want babies now, take a few years off and do that. You can always return to your training.

To sum it all up, keep your overhead low, play hard and take time to love those who love you. What else really matters?

Although I have laid bare the grim landscape of modern medical practice, it's not all bad. I had a great career. Most of my work was done in a small rural emergency room. Our staff was a close knit group. We had our spats and differences, but when someone truly ill came through the door, everyone dropped what they were doing and pulled the rope in the same direction. This included the head of maintenance. Whenever necessary, he would prop his broom against a wall, put on latex gloves and start chest compressions. The nurses that had been working there for years knew most of the families in town. They contributed invaluable insights into family dynamics. The police sergeant who had lived locally for ever, would call me up and say "Doc can you lend us a hand? Old George is a bit confused. He's walking down Main Street again in his underwear. What are we gonna do about this?"

Even though it's not part of a formal medical framework, the local town diner would send someone to check on their elderly regular customers if they did not show up for breakfast for two days in a row. If they found a problem at their customer's apartment, an ambulance was immediately called.

I never had to worry about my physician colleagues dropping the ball when following up on one of my patients. They were all intelligent and committed to good medical care. Our paramedics were unbelievable. A smoking car upside down in a ditch at 2:00 am in freezing weather was all in a day's work. They never backed down from a challenge.

We had a great dialogue with the local volunteer ambulances. We would provide them with continuing medical education. In return they would communicate any concerns they had about a patient. They also brought us photographs of serious automobile accidents. In terms of the mechanics of trauma injuries, one picture is indeed worth a thousand words.

In addition, I had the medivac helicopter and the poison control center backing me up twenty four hours a day. A small rural emergency room works great only if you can get critically ill patients to a proper trauma center or cardiac bypass center very quickly.

In short, it was community medicine the way it should be practiced. But what most people don't realize is that community medicine is on the endangered species list. As the individual states scramble to save money by consolidating medical care into large regional centers, community hospitals are increasingly seen as inefficient dinosaurs. We were constantly under threat of closing due to the lack of funding. In that atmosphere nursing moral suffers. It was difficult to keep a stable nursing staff. They all had families, and if they thought our facility was going to close, they went off looking for another job.

Like most situations in life, we have choices. As a patient you can be a number in a large medical machine, or you can be a patient in a place where they know your name. If the latter means anything to you, then it's time to join the fight to preserve community care. The small community hospitals will not survive without a consolidated and committed effort to lend support.

Occasionally the nurses and I would save a person's life. I don't say this to pat myself on the back. I say this to communicate that when someone is going over the edge of the cliff, there is nothing like reaching out, grabbing their outstretched hand and pulling them back. At the end of the day it doesn't get any better than that. During my cancer treatment some good people prolonged my life. It goes both ways.

Finally, my training as a professional counselor proved invaluable. You can never isolate physical disease from a patient's emotional state. You have to deal with both. Counseling skills must be part of any medical school curriculum. But the sensitivities necessary to do counseling work cannot be taught in a four week touchy/feely course. Those skills have to be woven within the fabric of the entire four years of medical training as well as residency. It's more than worth the effort.

Speaking of medical residency, late one night, deep within the bowels of the hospital, I penned the following. Don't ask me why!

WORLD MEDICAL NEWS

Coffee Dispenser Claimed As Panacea

Recently, worldwide attention has been focused on a Memphis Tennessee General Hospital. A coffee dispenser located outside the eighth floor orthopedic ward has reportedly been linked to a series of amazing healings.

The story began on the night of October 16th when a seventy year old maintenance worker by the name of Irvina Glatz put her coins into the machine. Irvina had a terribly deformed right hand, apparently the result of a childhood accident with a turnip shredder in Tuscaloosa, Alabama. As she reached out for the coffee, her right hand miraculously straightened. At first her story was not believed, but soon co workers and patients alike stood in line for the machine's miracles.

What has scientists even more bewildered is the fact that each beverage selection from the machine seems to heal a different ailment. Black coffee heals arthritis; coffee with cream, breast cancer; coffee with sugar, diabetes; coffee with cream and sugar, infertility; coffee with saccharin and no cream, dental caries; decaf coffee with extra sugar and minimal cream (in the green cup), blood disorders; hot chocolate with artificial marshmallows, hemorrhoids; and the chicken soup seems to moderately improve everything.

The machine's manufacturers are at a loss. "As soon as we heard of this", Instacup VP Maurice Gunther said, "We took a truck load of machines out to the Geyser Lake home for the disheveled, but all we got was coffee."

The Very Reverend Horatio Onslaught, of the Bathed in the Blood Baptists Brethren said "We cannot question the wondrous ways of the Lord!" He then allowed himself to be bitten by a coral snake in front of the machine. Unfortunately, an appropriate selection for snakebite could not be found. He was, however, able to survive in a semi vegetative state with the help of the chicken soup.

Wreaths and candles now surround the machine, giving a golden glow to the change return. An emergency generator has been placed to ensure a continuous power supply. Paper napkins containing spilled coffee from the machine are being mailed worldwide and are available with a prayer booklet and creamer. Also included is a short video tape of baptisms done during the flood season.

Where all this will end is unclear, but legislation is being drafted to enable Medicare to cover the rising cost of coffee.

Chapter XIV

POLITICALLY INCORRECT

Part One

Trust me. The opinions expressed in this chapter do not represent the official opinions of any place I ever worked. In fact, if the following observations on human behavior ever get published, I'll probably never be able to work as a physician again.

I fully understand that many of society's problems are extremely complicated. But rather than get bogged down in endless detail, the emphasis here will be on what we can do to make a bad situation better. That involves taking our collective heads out of the sand and looking at serious social problems head on. I'm not searching for over simplified answers. Instead I am searching for the will that motivates positive change.

One consistent thread that seems to run through most forms of sociopathic behavior centers on many people's unwillingness to connect their actions to the consequences of those actions. The carnage that results from their irresponsible lifestyles hurts us all. Irresponsible behavior can be either aggressive or passive. You can beat your wife, or just not provide for your family. I'm going to give these irresponsible life styles a collective name. I'm going to call this mode of existence "chaotic living". Chaotic living represents the opposite of being a team player. The damaging effects of pure selfishness go way beyond the boundaries of an individual life.

Perhaps the most obvious destructive lifestyles center around the problem of drug and alcohol abuse. The first essential insight into substance abuse is that the scope of the problem is far greater than realized by the general public. Let's face it, rather than focus on such an ugly side of life, most of us just choose to ignore the problem. That works until a loved one goes down to drugs or alcohol.

Here are a few statistics that will help clarify the scope of the problem. First of all, about one in seven American adults suffer from alcohol related issues. Roughly 19.5 million people in the U.S. use illegal drugs. Of those 19.5 million, 19,000 die each year as a direct result of their drug use. About another 22,000 die each year in alcohol related automobile accidents. Two million more people are injured. Switching over to the United Kingdom, at any given moment, 7% of the population is alcohol dependent. But here is the real clincher: About half the people in the U.S.A. who are severely injured in an accident have evidence of alcohol or drug impairment.

As a footnote, drug overdoses are frequently the result of ingesting both alcohol and multiple drugs. Sorting out what they have taken and treating each drug separately and appropriately can be a bit tricky. We have toxicology blood tests to help us with this, but those tests take time. Sometimes we just support ventilation and blood pressure any way we can, and sort out the details later. While the patient is being treated, the patient's family often goes absolutely crazy. Somehow they are surprised by all of this.

When treating drug addicts, there is also an inherent risk to E.R. personnel. No matter how many gloves we wore, or precautions we took, most of us have been stuck by dirty needles.

The drug or alcohol addict cares more about the objects of their substance abuse than they do about themselves, their spouse, their children, their home, their job, their self respect and society as a whole. What a joy it must be for those who love and depend on the addict to watch them change themselves from a functioning member of society into an unrelenting burden and source of constant worry and anxiety. Addiction represents the essence of negation, futility and turmoil. Each alcoholic adversely affects an average of five other people on a day to day basis.

Often addict's children have been organizing the family since their early years. Instead of a normal childhood, they live within a mammoth deception as the family tries to hide the addict's prolonged downward slide. Frequently the kids are targets of abuse. As a result, when they grow up, their own marriages tend not to do well. They have trouble making themselves vulnerable to other human beings. What makes things even worse is that the child of an alcoholic tends to hook up with a drug addict or alcoholic themselves. Why would a child who has been tortured psychologically by an addicted parent get into a similar relationship as an adult? They do it because they are so familiar with that situation. They know what to expect. They are used to it. Their pain defines them.

The addict's life becomes one unrelenting manipulative lie. An addict cannot walk up to someone on the street and say "Would you please pay for me to get higher than a kite tonight?" Instead they will walk up to a stranger and say "This is my baby," (actually the baby was borrowed from another addict. The baby is nothing more than a prop). "My baby has not eaten for days because I have no money. Would you give me some money so I can buy my baby some milk?" If you offer to walk them to the market so they can buy the milk directly, they will usually find some way to foil your plan. The money will never be used for baby's milk.

Obviously emergency medical work brought me into frequent contact with addicts. It was not uncommon on a given hospital day for me to see more patients presenting false signs and symptoms in order to get narcotics than it was for me to see patients presenting with genuine pain. The drug addict who is a beginner at abusing emergency rooms is easy to spot. His story really doesn't make medical sense. Often they give the triage nurse a different medical history than they give me, as if the nurse and I never talk to each other. But with time and practice the drug addict's routine becomes very polished. It's sometimes very difficult to tell who is lying and who is not. I know some days I got it wrong. I know that during some of my shifts, addicts walked out of the emergency room with narcotics, while people who had real pain walked out with non narcotic prescriptions. In the absence of visible disease or trauma it's impossible to prove whether a patient's pain is real or not. What made it really difficult was that both the patient with pain and the addict appeared desperate. The experienced addict can turn tears off and on like a faucet.

Desperate to get some sense of what was really going on with a patient I would often turn to the computer. With a little luck the computer would disclose that the patient had made several visits to local emergency rooms and clinics over the last few days requesting pain killers each time. I would then walk into the addict's treatment room and ask if they had seen any other medical professionals for this problem in the last forty eight hours. The answer was invariably "No".

Not infrequently addicts on welfare (a lot of addicts are on welfare because it's hard to hold down a 9-5 when you are high most of the time.) would canvass numerous doctors looking for pain medications. Health professionals call this activity "shopping". The state government who hands out the money for welfare prescriptions would occasionally send me a letter showing that I was one of four doctors writing for a patient's narcotics simultaneously. Often these numerous prescriptions would total hundreds of narcotic pills each month.

In addition there was never any concern on the addict's part that their fictitious illness might be taking me away from a complicated elderly sick patient who really needed a lot of my time. There was never any concern for anything but the drugs. I have seen tens of thousands of dollars spent on exotic x-ray and blood tests to work up illnesses that never existed in the first place. Often the physician has to work hard to get an expensive study scheduled for a welfare patient. Lots of E.R. and medical office time is spent on the phone arguing with insurance beaurocrats. But once the expensive study was scheduled, the patient rarely showed up. There is always an excuse, but the bottom line is that they know the study will be negative. A negative study makes it harder to get more narcotics. So they wail about their pain while the doctor gives them another narcotic prescription and tries to reschedule the x-ray study. This pattern repeats itself time and again. When the addict finally burns out the local health care system, they simply change their location and present themselves as helpless victims to a different and initially sympathetic emergency room.

There are indeed innocent victims within society, but not nearly as many as you would think. For example, an employee falls at work and develops chronic back pain. After a period of time he gets hooked on pain killers. I mean you have to feel sorry for him. But if you really probe the story, you find out that when he originally fell, he was drunk.

When I saw a patient come into the emergency room with medical records that were twelve inches thick, a five year old x-ray and an out of state license plate, I knew it was going to be a long night. Once in a while their medical problems were indeed real, but most often it was part of an elaborate scam. They usually came in at night or on the weekend when the doctor who originally signed their medical charts could not be found. Sometimes when I could (with much effort) find their doctor, I would say "I think your patient might be a drug seeker." That would be followed by a pause and "Yeah, you're probably right" or "We don't prescribe pain medication for that patient anymore." One scam was so elaborate and convincing that I flew the patient by helicopter to a level one trauma center. That's a five thousand dollar cab ride. It also made that helicopter unavailable for any other emergency cases for at least an hour. Occasionally I would call the helicopter for a patient who desperately needed a cardiac catheterization only to find out that both helicopters were tied up with other calls. The trauma center worked up my patient with two day's worth of expensive studies and multiple M.R.I. and C.T. scans before confronting him with his pain medication seeking behavior. He then pulled the I.V. out of his arm, jumped off the stretcher and walked out of the hospital with no sign of pain.

One good way to see if your patient is telling the truth about their pain is to watch them walk to their car after they leave the hospital. At least a third of the time, that horrible limp they had when they came to the hospital would miraculously vanish when they left. Also, if you have three patients seeking narcotics at the same time, see if they all leave the hospital in the same car.

On rare occasions I was just too tired to argue and wrote a narcotic prescription. Word would rapidly spread on the street that Dr Davisson was weak today and the waiting room would start to fill up.

Patients with a long drug abuse history would never stop trying for drugs, but their success rate diminished over time as they became more and more familiar to the local emergency room staff. As a result the addict would sometimes begin to bully his wife or girlfriend into faking an illness to get the pills. Over time the girlfriend often became addicted and co dependent.

Most of the burglaries and muggings in a given community are drug related. When brought to court, the addict is often given the option of going to a drug rehab program instead of going to jail. What a bad joke. Does anyone really think that being caught during a burglary is going to make the addict give up the drugs? His lawyer makes sure the addict looks good in court in a suit and tie. The addict is a professional manipulator and clearly knows how to song and dance the court. As the addict lays out his woeful story, tears will flow. If you read the trial testimony in the newspapers, the defense lawyer makes it sound as if the drugs, not the defendant, committed the crime. Let's get one thing straight: drugs and alcohol addict and disinhibit, but the person commits the violent crime. Just think about it. A lot of guys get roaring drunk on the weekend, come home and *don't* beat up their wives. If they do beat up their wives, it's because the alcohol has unleashed a brutal monster that was there *before* he started drinking. You must hold people responsible for what they do regardless of the standard excuses.

In the same breath I have to say that there is some evidence indicating that there is slightly less repeat drug related crime among felons that go to rehab instead of jail. But at the very least, those who are sent to rehab have to be carefully screened. Violent offenders need to go to jail. I've done the last minute history and physicals on these folk prior to admission to a rehab program. Nine out of ten had no interest in purging drugs and alcohol from their lives. They simply did not want to go to jail. They will play the requisite role while in the rehab program and never look back after they leave.

Another real problem is that places in good rehab programs are difficult to find for those without medical health insurance. If any rehab program takes on too many uninsured patients, they will go bankrupt. Save those valuable few available free rehab slots for patients who genuinely want to kick the habit, not for those who don't want to wake up behind bars.

I'll never forget taking care of a patient who was found unconscious in the middle of the road in broad daylight. No medical history was available. The ambulance crew properly collared and back boarded him and brought him to the emergency room. When I saw him, he was breathing without difficulty and had a normal pulse and blood pressure. His blood glucose was normal and his pupils were equal and reactive. The next step in evaluating him was a complete body survey for trauma. After all, he was found in the middle of the road. I helped the nurse completely undress him while an emergency medical technician maintained cervical traction in case he had a neck fracture. There was alcohol on his breath. There were no obvious signs of trauma or needle tracts. X-rays and blood work came back normal except for a grossly elevated blood alcohol level. We gave him some I.V. fluids that contained the vitamins alcoholics require and then let him sober up. But while I was undressing him I noticed that he had clean socks. This didn't fit the picture. People who drink enough to pass out in the middle of the road in broad daylight do not wear clean socks. They usually have been in the same clothes for weeks. After he sobered up, I had a chat with him to make sure that I didn't miss any serious medical conditions. As it turns out he had just been discharged from a thirty day alcohol detox program. His driver's license had been revoked so he walked home. On the way home he decided to stop and have just one drink with an old friend. The next thing he remembers is talking to me. That inpatient detox program cost thousands of dollars. He never even made it home.

Lots of people can get caught up in the addict's web of deception. For example, doctors themselves can become complicit with a patient's addictive behavior. Some doctors, functioning with the best of intentions, don the mantel of the rescuing angel. They love to gallop in on their white charger and restore order. Drug addicts are very sensitive to savior tendencies within physicians. They will play on the physician's sense of guilt when their "pain" doesn't get better. "Please doctor, I'm counting on you to help me. No one other than you seems to want to help me with my pain. You're my final hope." A really polished addict will play on the physician's guilt for years. After a prolonged period of time it's difficult for the physician to admit he was wrong. At that point it's far easier to give in to the addict's demands and keep writing prescriptions.

One of the favorite ploys used by addicts on new physicians is "If I go into a rehab program I might lose my job. Just give me the pills and I will detox at home." So the doctor writes out a week's worth of narcotic pills with careful instructions on how to decrease the dose each day until the patient is drug free. Two days later the addict is back in the doctor's office. "Doc, my brother in law stole my pain pills. You've got to help me."

Some liberal misguided individual might ask "Why not give the addict the pills he wants? Then everyone is happy." Here's why you don't do that:

No.1: Addicts do not take prescribed doses of narcotics. You can never be sure what will happen when you give them the pills. Say an addict has just taken enough extra strength Vicodin to render you and I unconscious. They then get into a car and drive. Your family and my family are out there on that same road. The addict never shows any concern for public safety. They will just tell the judge how sorry they truly are after they collide with and kill a family of four. They are sure they can turn their lives around if they could just get into a good rehab program.

No.2: Everyone has to make a living. The typical drug addict cannot or will not work, so they don't consume all of the two hundred narcotic pills that they managed to con out of three different physicians. Instead they save half the pills for themselves and sell the other half on the streets. A street pusher can get five to ten dollars apiece for the right pills. So it's very possible that a fourteen year old girl will be found in a coma and holding a pill container that has my name on it.

So what are the causes of this immense problem we call addictive behavior? Some clinician's argue that addicts turn to substance abuse in order to blot out terrible memories of being abused as children. It is indeed true that a lot of drug addicts and alcoholics were abused as kids. This is no huge surprise given that many of their parents are drug addicts or alcoholics. It's easy to target kids when there is that much unhappiness and frustration in the family. Other clinician's argue that there is an addictive gene; therefore the problem of addiction is genetic in origin. It is appropriate to classify drug and alcohol addiction as a disease because years of addiction will indeed lead to very real and predictable medical consequences. But notice what this kind of thinking does. It turns all of the drug addicts and alcoholics into innocent victims. As a health professional you have to think this way to some degree if you're going to work day in and day out with addicts. Otherwise the lies and manipulation alone would drive you crazy.

I've had alcoholics say to me "What I do is not my fault; I have a disease." Let's get one more thing straight. When a thirty four year old female with advanced terminal breast cancer wakes up in the morning, she tries to shake off the adverse affects of the poisonous chemotherapy she got yesterday. She somehow has to find the strength to get through one more day because she has three young children. She has very few choices. When a drug addict or alcoholic wakes up every morning, they have a very clear choice. They can go on spreading pain and chaos in the world or they can sober up. Going through drug or alcohol withdrawal is not a pleasant experience and should always be done under medical supervision. But every day of the week lots of people do it.

No matter what sad story the addict gives you about why they do the drugs or alcohol, after a number of years all that really matters to them is that they get high. Until they sober up, nothing good will happen. There is simply no substitute for sobriety.

One course of action that an addict's family can take is to apply "tough love" to the addict. The idea behind "tough love " is that the addict will sober up when they finally hit bottom (i.e. they are out on the street). Thus the family will do nothing to prevent the addict from experiencing the adverse affects of their downward slide. Sometimes this actually works. Suffering is a great motivator for behavioral change. But it's also important to understand that no matter how much tough love you give some addicts, they will take the alcohol or drugs until the addictive substance kills them. For some people there is no bottom. The hard truth is that nothing you can do or say will change their behavior. They have made an unfortunate terminal choice. I suggest emotionally distancing yourself from addicts who won't quit substance abuse. If you stay connected to these people, they will take you down with them.

Some of my close friends are recovering alcoholics. Listening to them is fascinating and instructive. Once they sober up, a few interesting things happen. First of all the lying stops. They have finally faced the truth about their addiction. Next, an air of true humility develops. They realize their own vulnerability to the drugs and/or alcohol. They also had to face their own inner demons in order to quit leaning on the drugs. In other words, they grew up.

Occasionally you meet an intelligent alcoholic who had real plans for their lives. Then they got lost in the booze. When they finally crawled out of the bottle twenty five years later, much of their life had passed them by. They lost that admission to graduate school. Their dreams turned to dust. Now all they have left is their current new job for which they are very grateful, and their A.A. meetings which they must attend. What a wakeup call. They also know that they can never go back to the way life was prior to the addiction. They will always be vulnerable to a relapse. That's why A.A. meetings are a lifelong commitment.

Speaking of Alcoholics Anonymous, whatever you think of their approach to alcoholism, they are the only organization that gets consistently good results. Support A.A. groups any way you can.

Speaking from a personal point of view, I've had a few very painful surgeries which required narcotic use. Initially, taking the narcotic pills was kind of fun. But after a while I noticed something sinister. Previously I mentioned that we all have an innermost center of emotional healing. I found that the narcotics cut me off from that center. My emotional receptors became flooded by the narcotic high. This led to mood swings. My ship had lost its rudder.

Going back to the subject of children and addiction, in the last few years of my medical career I noticed that a number of teenage addicts were also labeled with a diagnosis of manic depression. As stated before, manic depression is no joke. But I found myself questioning the diagnosis in a number of those cases. Granted, addiction is often part of a much larger personality disorder. But on a good day, the average teenager rides an emotional roller coaster. Take any teenager's brain and marinate it in drugs on a daily basis for years and you will see some pretty wild mood swings. As a result, teenage addicts often experience depression. It would be interesting to do a study on teenagers who have been off drugs for a few years. How many of them would still have symptoms consistent with a diagnosis of manic depression?

Finally, I want to make one additional small point regarding addiction. As previously stated kicking addiction requires facing the truth. As a colleague of mine once said "The truth is the only way forward." But take that idea one step further. Get to the point in life where the truth, not the drugs, is your friend.

Whatever you think of addiction, there is no avoiding the fact that it is supremely selfish. The addict essentially says "The whole world can go to hell while I get high." This was acutely illustrated when a doctor friend of mine made a house call to an addict's home. She got manipulated into giving the addict a benzodiazepam (Valium) prescription. The addict grabbed the prescription and set out on a fast walk to the nearest pharmacy. The addict's three year old son ran after him yelling "Daddy, Daddy!" But the addict never broke stride or turned around to acknowledge his son. The addict was going after what mattered most to him.

At this point I want to move the focus of our discussion away from the addict and instead take a careful look at those people who are emotionally connected to the addict. I've watched patients drink alcohol over the years to the point where they have permanent brain damage (Wernicke's encephalopathy). As a result, the alcoholic loses the coordination necessary to walk unaided. These people are essentially house bound. But regardless of the inability to ambulate, they still periodically turned up in my emergency room grossly intoxicated. This means that someone is bringing the drunk the alcohol that is slowly killing him. Now who would do that? The neighbors won't do it. They are sick and tired of the loud domestic arguments. Social services won't do it. After a hard day dealing with dead beats the social workers need the alcohol for themselves. The alcoholic's kids probably won't do it. They split from the chaotic household long ago. They only visit when they get the call from the emergency room or the police station. So, who throws gasoline on the roaring addictive fire? It's usually the spouse (or "significant other"), parents or grandparents. That's right folks, those closest to the carnage feed the flames. This type of behavior is called "enabling." What's really scary is that enabling behavior is very common. The odds are that anyone reading this page personally knows an enabler.

So how does an addict hook up with an enabler? Well, long term addiction really takes two to tango. The addict probably doesn't hold down a job; therefore they need someone to put food in their mouth and a roof over their head. As a result, the addict will cruise the local scene looking for the more vulnerable, willing and easily manipulated members of our society. Upon finding a likely candidate, the addict spins one pathetic yarn after another until the enabler becomes emotionally tangled up in the addict's lies.

The enablers themselves often come from addictive parents. They know clearly what is expected of them. The enabler's behavior gives us a valuable insight into what I will call the "realm of the familiar". People will stay in unbelievably painful relationships if they are used to that kind of pain. As stated before, their pain defines them. It's the devil they know. They are also aware that the addict will "crash" without them, therefore the enabler feels needed. It's their job to smooth over the bumps and keep the addictive ship afloat.

In addition to feeling needed, the enabler gets something out of living on a razor's edge. They are constantly worried about whether their drunken husband will come home tonight and beat the kids, or whether the bank will foreclose on the house, or how in the world the enabler can find the strength to work a full time job, clean the house and raise the kids by herself. She is also really worried because she's just found three empty vodka bottles under her fifteen year old daughter's dirty laundry. Living in this constant state of anxiety provides its own adrenalin rush. Some enablers seem to feed on that rush.

A slight variation on the theme occurs when a teenage boy gets out of an inpatient drug rehab program. When he gets home, his grandmother looks at him and says "You really could use a new shirt." She reaches inside her purse and pulls out some cash. Placing the money in his hand, she says "Go down to Ed's Clothing Store and get yourself a decent shirt". The amount of money she places in his hand is exactly what he needs to get his next fix on the street. It's all about returning to the status quo.

More than anything else, enabling behavior says volumes about the enabler's self image. People with a strong self image would never put up with the emotional garbage the addict hands out. Often the enabler feels guilty about some real or imagined past event. The addict knows just how to push those guilt buttons.

In summary, the phenomenon of addictive behavior rarely affects the addict in isolation. The poisonous roots of addiction reach far and wide. The horrible consequences of these destructive lifestyles can go on for generations.

Once again on a personal note, towards the end of my career I began to feel used. The addicts know that all they have to do is fall backwards and a huge public service safety net will catch them. A combination of the emergency medical and social services personnel will perform what could be seen as enabling behavior. The emergency team picks the addict up off the street, dusts them off and fixes them as much as possible. Social services then find the patient a warm and dry bed and counseling. All of this costs a lot of tax payer's money. A month later the same addict is once again found in the emergency room; only now there is a newly issued arrest warrant as well as a new baby on the way. The ripple effects of addictive behavior continue unabated and the care givers help it go on.

What's the answer to this overwhelming and expensive endless loop? Beats me. I guess all we can do as health professionals is to try to help people get better.

One final word on addiction. Human beings are creatures of habit. We find comfort in our routines; it's one way we deal with life's stressors. Once we get into a particular habit over a long period of time, it can be very difficult to change that behavior pattern. Therefore as time goes on, be very careful about which habits you adopt.

As children go through their turbulent teenage years, they are very vulnerable to the acquisition of addictive habits. Often their need to belong to a peer group outweighs their common sense. In fact, if you want to deliberately ruin a teenager, here's how to do it. No matter what the teenager does, no matter how terrible their actions, shield them from the consequences of those actions. Regardless of how antisocial their behavior, they are still your little Johnny or Susie and everything will be O.K. Actions have consequences. If you remove that lesson from a child's life, their development arrests at a very primitive state. In fact, if you protect kids in this manner consistently over the years, I can almost guarantee your child will grow up to be an addict or criminal or at the very least a continuous burden on society. At that point all you can hope for is that some major traumatic life event will wake them up.

One additional problem is that kids today aren't afraid of anything. Corporal punishment has been removed from public schools. You even have to be careful what you say to the kids. Schools are scared to death of lawsuits because they haven't got the time or funds for a long court battle. This situation reduces the teacher to a position of minimal authority. What really needs to happen to many young boys is to have a drill sergeant in charge of them for a year. Issues would get sorted so quickly. For one thing the child would develop a sense of self respect, which is the biggest safeguard against childhood addiction. I realize that the boot camp solution to teenage problems won't work for everyone, but it beats the approach of raising kids without boundaries.

Antisocial behavior is by no means limited to addiction alone. Addiction is just the most obvious tip of the antisocial iceberg. If you look at the major text books on mental illness you will find that each particular psychiatric malady has a very precise designation. For instance manic depressive illness is DSM 296.63, oppositional defiant disorder is DSM 313.81 and paranoid schizophrenia is DSM 295.30.[2] These well defined labels for mental illness serve two functions:

No.1: If a patient is consistently treated for a very precise diagnosis, the treatment will be informative. If the treatment doesn't work then a new or additional diagnosis needs to be considered. If the treatment does work then you know that you and the patient are moving in the right direction. The confusion that results from a sloppy diagnosis can lead to considerable delays between the initial evaluation and the patient receiving effective help.

No.2: Mental health facilities are always going out with cap in hand looking for funding. Many of their patients cannot or will not work and thus cannot pay for their treatment. Insurance companies and government agencies are slow to reimburse the care givers unless the patient has a very precise diagnosis. Thus all of the insurance providers require that those diagnosing numbers be included on their reimbursement forms.

The only problem with this system is that it lacks a DSM R.S.B. designation for rotten selfish bastard. There are a lot of really irresponsible people and society has lost the ability to censor their behavior. Unless you break a major law in western societies, you can pretty much do whatever you want and no one will say a word. You can't even call anyone "bad" anymore. For example, you can't say anyone is "selfish"; they instead have a "narcissistic personality disorder". No one is a "thief"; they just have "poor impulse control." Likewise, no one is "violent." Those poor souls have "anger management issues." The nomenclature has been manipulated to water down the impact of what bad people do. The whole current approach to malevolent human behavior is to be non judgmental. Granted, some people have problems because they are just not wired right. But removing people from the

[2] *Diagnostic and Statistical Manual of Mental Disorders DSM-IV-TR Fourth Edition, Copyright 2000, American Psychiatric Association pp. 100,313,348*

adverse feedback resulting from their actions has no affect other than to increase their anti-social behavior.

When I was at seminary, the poor were seen as unfortunate victims of a society run by big business and big government. In essence, "big" was "bad". Without question corporate greed knows no bounds and government has to be watched every step of the way. Institutional corruption is endemic. But having said that, years in the emergency room have taught me that the most rabid, irresponsible and downright pernicious behavior rests with selfish and manipulative individuals. For example, some men will father four or five children by different women and abandon each of them without a second thought. As soon as they get bored or get a better offer, they are gone. What's going to be the quality of those abandoned kids upbringing? It will be marginal at best. Those children have little chance of escaping poverty, violence, drugs and alcohol.

Let's get another thing straight; in order to be called a "father" a man has to put in the time and money with the kid. If you are not willing to perform those basic tasks, then you are not a "father"; you are instead a "sperm donor". There is a huge qualitative difference between the two.

Recently two thirteen year old girls entered a local emergency room. They handed their babies to the grandmothers (aged 30 and 32 respectively) and whipped out their pocket computer games. In emergency medicine we call this situation "babies having babies." Reportedly the sperm donors were gang members, so I am not sure how much choice the girls had about their pregnancies. One of the prevailing cultures says that if you have been with your woman for a while and she hasn't had a baby, then you're not a real man. This kind of immature thinking has to change. What possible chance do those babies have?

I've taken care of pregnant women who have had their last four or five children removed by social services due to "inadequate parenting". "Inadequate parenting" means anything from abandonment to abuse. A few years ago I dealt with one such lady. She was really happy because she was pregnant *again*. But this time her man was going to stand by her. We all said "congratulations." We then went into the nurse's lounge, closed the door and cried.

Mother Nature couldn't give a squat about whether or not a pregnant woman will be a good mother. Fertility has nothing to do with maternal competence. A lot of women can't even take care of themselves. What do you think will happen when they have a baby? Who do you think will be the focus of their sense of frustration and inadequacy? The best the baby can hope for is to be abandoned and placed in institutional care.

This brings us to my one big quarrel with the anti-abortion groups. Who is going to pick up the pieces after the unwanted baby is born? The cliché "The baby will be adopted", is inadequate. There may be a line forming to get healthy white babies, but what about minority babies or babies with real physical problems who are often born to drug addicted mothers? Who is going to care for them?

Personally, having my own child has changed the way I look at abortion. I could not order an abortion unless the fetus was seriously damaged, the mother's life was in danger or the fetus was the result of a rape. (If the conception was the result of a rape, then there is a good chance that the new mother will make the baby pay for the rape. Don't look for rationality in these situations). But whether you are pro life or pro abortion, if you are not doing everything possible to prevent unwanted teenage pregnancy, then you are a hypocrite. You cannot take abortion as an issue and isolate it from the myriad social problems surrounding teen pregnancy. And don't give me that born again "teach abstinence" crap. On a grand scale that has never worked and it never will.

While in residency I took care of a woman who could only be described as a lump. She wasn't mean. She wasn't out to hurt anyone. But she was completely willing to give up all responsibility for her life. So she had to be clothed, fed and led through life's daily obligations. But she did manage to do one thing. She had five illegitimate kids by five different sperm donors. The sperm donors themselves were not Nobel Lauriat's. As a consequence three of the five children had severe personality disturbances and will be under care of the state for most of their lives. But it doesn't stop there. Her fifteen year old boy was having random indiscriminate sexual contact with underage girls. I asked him "Are these girls you're having sex with on birth control?" He looked at me and said "What's that?"

The irresponsible behavior of fertile human beings lands babies in terrible situations. To start with, look at the effects of cocaine use on early fetal brain development. Or how about the joy of a new born baby going through heroin withdrawal? What a great way to introduce a new baby to life! Did I mention fetal alcohol syndrome? (Fetal alcohol syndrome is a constellation of signs and symptoms that develop when a pregnant woman is drinking during fetal development. The most serious long term effect on the fetus is mental retardation.) Oh, and don't forget the transmission of sexually transmitted diseases to the fetus. And what about the lifelong effects of children being raised by those with marginal or malevolent parenting skills? Through all this carnage no one says a word about right or wrong; so these intense and frequent tragedies are doomed to repeat themselves.

This is not, however, a static situation. Say a woman has three damaged kids as a result of the above. There are about 4,500 emergency rooms in the United States. Those emergency rooms care for widely divergent patient populations. But it would not be unreasonable to estimate that each local emergency room cares for an average of two hundred seriously socially disadvantaged kids. That's 900,000 kids with immense needs who will require repeated intervention by emergency departments and social services. Now take those 900,000 unfortunate children and walk through the math when each of them has an average of two to five kids. Not every one of those kids will have serious problems, but a large percentage of them will. Then follow the expanding number of damaged kids through the next four generations and you will get some sense of where society is headed. One of my fears is that eventually those with pronounced social needs will grossly outnumber those trained to take care of them. And where's the money going to come from to deal with all this?

After a very difficult day in the emergency department, one of my nurses lost it. She told a pregnant welfare patient "You *can't* have another baby because *I* can't afford it!" You have to admit there is some logic to her statement. If someone decides to have a baby that they cannot support, why are the nurse's tax dollars paying for the consequences of that irresponsible decision? If I make a bad decision, the consequences of that decision rest squarely on my shoulders. Why doesn't this simple principle apply to everyone? The nurse was sent for sensitivity training.

Near where I first lived in England, thirty percent of the kids in the local town's grade school were on the "At Risk" register. That means the home situation for those kids was so bad that it presented a clear and present danger to the children. Can you imagine those kid's behavior in school? The school's guidance counselor would walk into the family practitioner's office and burst into tears. The guidance counselor's situation was hopeless. How was she supposed to deal with that mess? The government made lots of noise, spent money and ran in circles, but never really dealt with the human behavior that spawned such a chaotic and tragic situation.

This brings up another point. Politicians are quick to blame the large scale antisocial behavior of kids on inadequate schooling. Rubbish! Ninety percent of the problem of antisocial behavior lies in the kid's chaotic homes. Politicians blame the schools because schools don't vote, but parents do. Now hear this: schools cannot provide what inadequate parenting fails to provide. Repeat that ten times to yourself until that concept really sinks in. Should we work to improve our schools? Absolutely. But bad schools are just an extension of a rotting society. The schools provide a stage for the behavior of dysfunctional families.

I think people should be required to have a license in order to have a child. At first this sounds like a really bad joke, but think about it. You need a license to get married or drive a car. You even need a license to kill a fish. But when it comes to the most important decision in anyone's life, the decision that will have immense consequences for both the parents and society, more than half the time pregnancies are unplanned. A license to have a child would be almost impossible to enforce, and in the land of the free and home of the American Civil Liberties Union, this concept will never fly. But what do drug addicts, alcoholics, psychotics, antisocial personalities with violent tendencies, and just plain lazy good for nothing women all have in common? They are all mothers. Like it or not the schools, society and the tax payers have to deal with the consequences of their inability to adequately parent.

Outside of pregnancy, what other critical decision in life would anyone make in such a casual manner? One phrase that used to drive me crazy kept recurring in my emergency room. Whenever I had a female patient of child bearing age, I had to know whether or not she was pregnant. This was because the majority of medications I used in the acute setting could harm a fetus. When I got a history involving unprotected sexual intercourse I would say to the woman, "So, you're trying to get pregnant?" Time and again the female patient would turn to me and say "Well, we are not trying to have baby, but if it happens, it happens." The significant other sperm donor would sit in the corner with a sheepish grin on his face. Let's get one final thing straight. If you are having unprotected sexual intercourse, you are trying to have a baby. There is no way to water down that reality. So why the word game? The only thing I can think of is that the female is trying to not scare the male away. After all, they are not *trying* to have a baby. In other words, it might not really happen, so they don't have to look the sobering realities of child rearing squarely in the face.

Some women seem to look on a baby as a down payment on a long term relationship. Ladies, here's a hint. If the male is not willing to give his last name to the baby, then smart money suggests that he is not in for the long haul. Men need to have sex, then they need to leave.

Many sexually active women are involved with men who have a substance abuse problem, or are too emotionally unstable to hold down a job. If that is your situation, then you need to ask yourself, do you really want his D.N.A. in your child? The resulting baby might be beautiful, but it will also be half him.

Here's a novel concept. Two people of a reasonable age get married because they want to spend the rest of their lives with each other. Both of them train to get marketable skills and over time put a little money in the bank. Then the wife takes time off from work and has a baby. Later on the father may spend time at home as well, depending on their work situation. Why is this such an improbable scenario? A baby is something to have when life is rich and full, not just because it seems like a fun idea. No matter how you cut it, raising children properly is a lot of hard work.

What we have done is taken teenage girls, many of whom are society's least qualified people from an economic and psychological point of view, and paid them to have babies. Then we have the audacity to be surprised when, after a couple of generations, our collective ship of society runs aground.

In England, not only do unwed mothers get the monthly check, they are also eligible for a fully furnished apartment. This situation is a very viable career option for those who haven't got what it takes to pursue a skill or higher education. But recently a physician who works with unwed mothers made an interesting observation. She said "Sam, the unwed mothers aren't happy." I said "What do you mean?" She said "You can see them pushing their prams (baby carriages) and smoking their fags (cigarettes) in the town center, but in reality, they have given up all control over their own lives. For example, if social services houses them over a fish and chip shop with drug deals going down in the back alley, the unwed mothers really don't have much recourse." Obviously if someone else is paying your expenses, they will call the tune to which you have to dance.

There is another reason why a lot of unwed mothers are unhappy. Many of them are themselves targets of abuse. Not too far from the hospital where I used to work, some good people put together a shelter for battered women. That shelter is very busy. One frustrating aspect of dealing with battered women is that they often return home to the abuser. Part of the problem is the woman's poor self-image. Many of those women were themselves battered children. The classic pattern is that the abuser will offer profuse apologies, bring flowers and promise to never to do it again. That works until the next time he gets drunk and beats her up.

Other women leave the shelter and go home out of pure fear. They have been told "If you leave and take my kids, I will find you and kill you." Those women believe the threats are real. Police restraining orders applied to violent males are helpful, but remember, the police can only jail the abuser *after* the restraining order has been violated. Often, that's a bit too late. Support your local battered women's shelter. They desperately need your help.

Now let's turn our attention back to children from disadvantaged backgrounds. Every Pediatric Advanced Life Support course, which is a requirement for emergency room doctors and nurses, has a section on detecting child abuse. Why is there such emphasis placed on this painful subject? The reason for that emphasis is that if a battered child is brought to the emergency department and the E.R. staff misses the fact that the physical abuse was intentional, then there is a fifteen to twenty five percent chance that the child in question will someday return to the emergency room permanently physically disabled or dead. Deliberate abuse is very rarely an isolated single event. Child abuse is a pattern of behavior.

Social Services are always desperately searching for good and reliable foster homes for abused children. Taking care of these kids is often a difficult task. The children themselves are damaged goods, often acting out their fear, anger and frustration.

Another interesting form of abuse occurs when those who know they are infected with H.I.V. go out and have unprotected sexual intercourse with as many people as they can. This is truly assault with intent to kill. Due to medical confidentiality doctors and nurses can say nothing. We just look at each other, shake our heads, grab a donut for comfort and get on with the day.

The elderly also line up for their fair share of abuse. When I was a student in the South Bronx, gangs of teenagers would regularly mug the elderly. The gang members called the old people "Candy" because they were so easy to rob (It was like taking candy from a baby). If the elderly victim had little or no money, a gang member would shoot or stab them in the arm or leg to remind them to carry more money next time. This is a form of terrorism. This was also before New York City put zero tolerance into effect.

Then there are the self-abusers. Confronted with any one of life's numerous stressors, they will cut their wrists (never deep enough to be life threatening) overdose on drugs that they *think* are benign, or throw themselves down in a crowded supermarket and fake a seizure. You can argue endlessly about the causes of such behavior. But when all is said and done, their behavior constitutes a very immature form of manipulation. Often these people go on to have children. You can imagine how well that works out.

Another pattern of abusive behavior that just boggles the mind involves women who had been badly abused as children. Upon growing into adulthood these women sometimes get involved in relationships where their own kids become targets of physical or psychological abuse. These mothers know their children are being abused, but say nothing. They are quietly complicit in the violence directed at their own kids. I suspect these women want the whole world to know how badly they have been hurt, so they re-enact that pain through their own sons and daughters. I could be very wrong on this, but I cannot think of any other motivation for such bizarre behavior. It's not like these mothers don't know how much abuse hurts.

Variations on the theme of abusive behavior are almost endless. Back home in the Midwest, I was working the night shift when the police brought in a man who had been a victim of ritualistic slicing with knives.

He was clean and reasonably dressed, and while his wounds needed attention, none were life threatening. I washed out and sutured his lacerations, gave him a tetanus shot, antibiotics and follow-up instructions. When the wound care was completed I asked him why he had allowed himself to be the target of such a methodical and malicious assault. All of the facts I could gather suggested that he was a willing participant in this late night ritual. He looked at me and said "I believe my blood is a sacrifice that God really wants" I was momentarily staggered by his statement. There was no evidence of psychosis, thought disorder, fragmented thinking, acute depression or intoxication. He was completely lucid. I had just met my first true masochist. He was not in any acute reversible mental state. There is no medication for his thought processes, although in retrospect, I bet his childhood was not standard issue.

In the midst of an emergency room's madness I did find one thing refreshing. I was continually being exposed to a real slice of life. I could not possibly have made up the events related in these pages, although I have altered the details to protect the patient's identity. All of the clichés about reality fall to pieces in the face of the events seen during a busy twelve hour shift in the emergency room. It really is life in the raw. It may be frustrating, disgusting, heart breaking or exhilarating and rewarding. But whatever it is, it is real.

Despite the huge numbers of abused and abusing adults, damaged children and manipulating addicts, it's difficult for a lot of people to admit just how bad things really are. The simple proof of the pudding is that any town of any size has to have its own police department. There are enough bad and whacked out people to necessitate that enormous expenditure of time and money. Speaking of which, when was the last time you thanked a cop? They are the only presence that prevents your house from becoming an armed fort. They deal with society's scumbags each and every day so that we are spared that experience. They are expected to perform in a flawless manner including making split second life and death decisions. Often their marriages do not go well. They have to protect themselves every day from the dregs of society. That can make being vulnerable in a marriage difficult. The police officer's spouse also has to deal with the daily fear of their loved one getting shot or stabbed.

A good police officer is a pillar in any community and a far cry from the "pig" designation given them back in the 1960s.

Getting back to the subject of society's disfunctionality, many folk rarely overtly break the law, but still manage to bring society to its knees. In the never ending affirmation of individual freedom, we've lost sight of something very important. We've lost sight of the common good. Day after day in the emergency room I saw an almost unending stream of people whose actions had negative and painful consequences for everyone else. We have given rise over the years to folk who will do whatever they want, whenever they want, regardless of the consequences to others. After all, each of them feels that they are doing *their* thing. The idea that *their* thing might have a far reaching negative impact on the rest of society just does not occur. Instead of taking responsibility for their actions, they will suck from the tit of social services day after day, without any thought of ever giving anything back.

One day I made a visit to the local soup kitchen which worked out of the town's Episcopal church. Week after week that organization fed a lot of people. In the yard in front of the kitchen stood two able bodied men about forty years old, each having a cigarette. All they could talk about was how bad the food tasted. That conversation represented the classic mentality of the loser. Did they help prepare the food? Nope. Did they say "thank you" for the only hot meal they will get that day? Unlikely. Were they helping with the clean up? Not a chance. But they were in the line for free food yesterday, and they will be in that same line tomorrow. Actually, their dialogue said more about their own self image than anything else.

A friend of mine did hard manual labor all of his life. Finally his back gave out resulting in frequent and intense pain. But he had to keep working. His son was severely brain damaged in a car crash, so his wife couldn't work because she cared for their son at home. Of course my friend had to pay taxes on what he earned. His blood was on every tax dollar he paid the government. The government then turned around and gave those tax dollars to the many able bodied welfare recipients that walked into our hospital. What's wrong with this picture?

An interesting twist occurs with many welfare patients. After they manage to manipulate the system and get onto the welfare roles, a kind of lethargy sets in. Little problems become big problems and anxiety and depression become common place. My point is that not working is not healthy. When life nears its end and you're sitting on the porch of the old folk's home, many people look back on their lives. If you've never invested your life in anything, if you've never drawn a line in the sand and made a stand, when it's all said and done, what have you got?

It would be unfair and untrue to say that everyone on welfare is a selfish and lazy person. The other side of the story centers on patients with terrible and progressive diseases. These people must have our help. In addition, life is tough and some folk, even on their best day, cannot deal with the stresses of daily existence. Those people also need our help. In a society relatively as rich as ours (I say relatively because no nation in history has ever had a national debt even vaguely approaching the debt burden of the United States), no one should starve to death. Soup kitchens and food banks provide a vital service. Not only do they minister to the down and out, they also serve families who are between jobs or who have been sidelined for a prolonged period by unexpected illness or trauma. If the uninsured drunk slams into your car late at night, who's going to show up for work while you're broken bones heal? Who's going to carry the ball when the pain from your ruptured disc gets so bad you have to go to the refrigerator on your hands and knees? If a family has small kids, things can get financially very difficult very quickly. An energetic local food bank can temporarily put food on children's plates that would otherwise go empty.

Besides not starving to death, no one in a wealthy nation should freeze to death. On some winter nights the cardboard box just isn't enough. In Washington D.C., The Community for Creative Non Violence has done some great work with the homeless. The nation's capital is no stranger to homeless people. During winter time, every warm air vent has a resident. The C.C.N.V. used to go around with a van and escort homeless folks to the shelters when temperatures plummeted to dangerous levels.

Why did the homeless not go to the shelters themselves (assuming they were not too high or drunk to move)? The homeless were hesitant to go to the shelters because there was a very real security risk. Not only might another shelter resident rip off what the few things they had, occasionally a psycho would get hyped up on an amphetamine analogue and start stabbing people. The shelters were run on shoestring budgets and could not provide adequate security services. There was always the danger that if anyone got hurt in a shelter due to inadequate security, that shelter could get sued.

The C.C.N.V. also used to go through supermarket disposal bins looking for food that they would cook for the homeless. Most of the food thrown out by supermarkets because the food was past its "sell by date" is still perfectly safe to eat. Initially the supermarkets turned a benevolent blind eye to this activity. But then someone (probably a lawyer) informed the supermarkets that they could be sued if anyone got sick from eating their disposed products. Soon afterwards, padlocks appeared on the disposal bins.

In addition to the down and outs, there is another group that definitely makes the endangered species list. That group is composed of working poor families. At the end of the month these people don't have enough money for proper health or dental insurance. A lot of businesses now prefer to hire part time employees in order to avoid the high cost of worker benefits. The working poor families get by until someone gets ill or their teeth rot due to lack of dental care. One worthwhile action would be for the government to pay about ten to ninety percent of the cost of health insurance for working poor families, depending on their income. Why should the guy who spends every day pushing the broom be worse off than the welfare recipient who sits at home doing nothing?

(Addendum March, 2010. Obamacare has just been passed. Instead of a simple subsidy for working poor families' health care insurance, what's been created is a 2000 page behemoth. It's so complicated that I'm not even sure how it's going to work.

My primary concern centers around Obamacare's financial viability. The National Health Service of England has had since the end of World War II to iron out its kinks. But with a U.S.A. national debt hovering around thirteen trillion dollars, I don't think Obamacare has that kind of time. One solution that has been offered is to pull money out of Medicare. That cannot be allowed to happen. All of the U.S. baby boomers are now becoming geriatric patients. Internal medicine and family practice offices cannot survive a big hit on Medicare reimbursement. This is one situation where you truly cannot rob Peter to pay Paul.

I sincerely hope a U.S. National Health Care system will work. All of Europe seems to have figured out the basics of the problem. Why can't the most powerful country in the world do the same?)

Another group that deserves a helping hand is working poor mothers. They should have subsidized child minding. What's the point of working if sixty percent of what they earn goes to the babysitter? If you want to get people off the welfare rolls, you have to make working worth their effort.

Outside of laziness, the fundamental reason that so many folks stay on their Medicaid rolls is that they don't want to lose their free Medicaid health insurance. But there is irony in this situation as well. The state health insurance is almost worthless. It will cover all of your emergency room visits and basic pediatric care, but that's it. Whenever I tried to arrange non emergent follow up care for a welfare patient I hit a brick wall. It's not that the medical specialists were unfeeling money grabbing monsters languishing on their yachts. A lot of them would take deserving community members under their wing, sometimes visiting the elderly in their homes. The problem was the enormous cost of running a modern medical practice. Add to this the huge expense of malpractice insurance and practices would go broke if they took on a significant number of welfare patients. The Medicaid welfare insurance payout for services rendered is simply inadequate. Basic economics only allows a limited amount of charity. Furthermore, as previously mentioned, the wide range of antisocial behavior that often accompanies the welfare patient creates real headaches for those involved in their treatment. Taking care of welfare patients can make a doctor's already difficult day a lot harder.

I remember one nurse practitioner whom I can only describe as "Mother Teresa the II." She organized a clinic for our local poor folk. It was a money loser, but an absolute necessity. Practitioners who worked there burned out quickly, but at least an avenue of care was provided.

Another huge health care problem for the poor centered around finding free dental care. For reasons just stated, none of the local dentists would take on welfare patients. Our state university school of dentistry *had* to take welfare patients because the school received state funding. Also, the dental school residents needed patients on which to sharpen their skills (so to speak). But the university was twenty miles away and usually their free clinics were booked up weeks in advance. I saw a lot of patients with dental pain. About twenty five to thirty five percent of them were drug seekers. Some of them would jab their gums with needles prior to being seen by me so that the area in question would appear inflamed. But for those with real dental pain, the situation was very frustrating. I could make them feel better with antibiotics and pain killers, but I couldn't solve the cause of their discomfort. Only a dentist could do that, and most of the time dental care was just not available.

Often I would look inside a mouth and see a row of black rotten stumps where teeth used to be. That's tragic, but how much effort and organization does it take to brush and floss twice a day to prevent those black stumps from occurring? Good dental hygiene is another reason why kids need to be raised in organized and responsible households.

While we are on the topic of acute emergency medical and dental care, let's get another final thing straight. No one in the United States who enters a public emergency room needing medical care gets turned away due to lack of money. Anyone who tells you differently is a liar. In the USA any hospital that takes state or federal funding is mandated to treat all comers. Personally, we always gave the most obnoxious, filthy, foul mouthed, violent, inconsiderate, manipulative, abusive, demanding, drunken and ill mannered patient the best care we knew how to give. We did not enjoy the experience. Our rate of doughnut consumption increased during those times. But we always did what we knew we had to do. The same is true for our pre hospital ambulance teams who, by the way, also delivered our doughnuts.

In summary then, no one should starve or freeze to death. In addition there should be a government sponsored subsidy for the working poor's health and dental insurance and child minding needs. Be honest. Wouldn't you rather see some money going to help poor families instead of being paid to those rich bastards who have run up trillions of dollars of bad debt and put our economy on the edge of a worldwide meltdown? But having said this, any government effort that goes beyond providing the basic services just mentioned, often unintentionally destroys human initiative. Any policy that destroys human initiative over the long term will turn out to be a very costly mistake. Doing nothing is a learned life style, and governments should not be running courses that teach that type of behavior.

Years ago I was taking in the scene next to the Washington monument in Washington D.C. There were lots of homeless people who sat motionless, like bushes on a landscape, providing a contrast to the fast moving tourists. One fellow in particular caught my attention. He was filthy and obviously had a substance abuse problem. But instead of sitting still, he was riding a large tandem bicycle. Bolted to each side of his bicycle were a total of four garbage cans. It was the middle of the summer and discarded soda cans were everywhere. He methodically collected the cans and flattened each one to the size of an envelope. He then tossed the soda cans into one of his large garbage receptacles. At five cents each for redemption, I figured that each garbage can held about twenty dollars worth of recyclable soda cans. This guy's life was a complete mess. But in the midst of his personal chaos, he still found a way to make something work.

POLITICALLY INCORRECT

Part Two

One area that is full of unique and isolating social problems is the inner city. Local emergency rooms reflect the chaos and madness of those communities. E.R. physician burn out is accelerated in that environment. The pay back for working in the inner city is how much you learn about trauma and advanced illness in a relatively short period. Only a war zone can expose a physician to more mortality and morbidity.

To make things worse, ghetto gangs rule the streets. Here's how it works. A twelve year old boy walks down the street. He is approached by several older gang members. They beat him up. He then asks "Why did you beat me up"? They say "Because you're not a member of the gang." The young man realizes that if he is going to live in that neighborhood, he will need to join a gang in order to survive. So he goes through the required membership rituals and becomes a gang member. He now has a greater sense of identity, which was not available from his chaotic home. After all, at his last birthday party, all the kids came over to his house and played hide and seek. One of the kids hid in the closet and discovered a dead body. There's no place like home.

A few weeks after joining the gang, he is approached on the streets by the same boys who then proceed to beat him up again. He asks "Why did you do that?" The answer comes back "You didn't pay your gang member dues." He asks "How much are the dues?" They give him a number. He says "I don't have that kind of money." They say "Don't worry; we're going to give you a job. Out of your wages you can pay your dues and have enough left for pocket money." "Great", he says. "What do I have to do?" He then becomes a drug runner for the gang.

The gang members know that if he gets caught, he will be tried as a juvenile. As long as the gang uses minors for their more visible drug activity, the overall risk of jail time for the older gang member infrastructure is reduced. (My gratitude to police officers who work with inner city gangs. They were the source of this information).

But every form of refuge has a price tag. The gang members I treated in the South Bronx were truly lost. I have no other words to describe their situation.

Perhaps the scariest reality to come out of the ghetto is the following: If a black youth commits murder, is caught and sentenced to death, he will probably outlive the fellow gang members he left behind in his neighborhood. The appeals process prior to execution will go on for years, maybe even decades. But the violence in the ghetto is unrelenting. It chews up more black youth every day.

A female paramedic friend of mine answered an inner city call for a domestic abuse victim. She arrived on the scene and found a woman standing alone outside in the dark. She had indeed been beaten up by her boyfriend, but was having trouble deciding whether or not to go to the hospital. As my friend tried to talk the woman into getting into the ambulance, the boyfriend appeared out of the shadows and put a gun against my friend's head and pulled the trigger. The gun didn't go off. The boyfriend started to laugh. The ambulance driver got out, threw both women into the back of the ambulance and sped off as fast as he could. That was the end of my friend's inner city career.

Ghetto violence will never diminish as long as there is big money in selling illicit drugs. Most of the violence centers on turf wars concerning who controls access to the drug buying public. For that reason alone, hard drugs should be legalized. That's not an easy stance for me to take, but nothing else outside of drug legalization will reduce the carnage in the inner city. In addition, systematic distribution of clean needles would dramatically reduce the incidence of Hepatitis B, Hepatitis C, H.I.V. and bacterial heart infections. These diseases in themselves are a major source of suffering.

But the illicit drug problem extends far beyond the drug users themselves. It is not uncommon for a relatively innocent person to get sexually involved with someone who has a history of I.V. drug use. The I.V. drug user then acts as a means of transmission for one of the terrible illnesses just discussed. That disease or diseases then get passed onto others including future offspring. I once worked in a V.D. clinic. You should see the look on people's faces when I tell them how many sexually transmitted diseases I will be testing them for over the next six months. Those patients and all of their prior sexual contacts then have to sweat it out until the test results come back. If I am dealing with a woman who has had sexual contact with someone who might have a sexually transmitted disease, I always throw in a pregnancy test. You can't be too careful.

Let's face it, we are losing the war on drugs. A few years ago I found myself asking "Why should one good D.E.A. agent die to keep people from doing to themselves what they want to do in the first place?" Government agencies might temporarily dry up the supply of hard drugs, but that supply will always return. There's just too much money to be made by supplying those drugs.

Take some of the enormous amount of money spent chasing the drugs and instead invest it in trying to prevent addictive behavior in the first place. Create a semester long course on the effects of illicit drug use. For seasoning, throw in the connection between hard drugs and sexually transmitted diseases. Make attendance to that course required for all twelve year olds. You don't even have to moralize while you teach the kids. Just explain to the students how the drugs and resulting diseases affect the human body. Then show them slide after slide that illustrates the health consequences of hard drug use to both the drug users and their sexual partners. A few slides showing what happens to users of crystal meth should be particularly effective. Such a visual presentation will without doubt have an impact on the kids.

A lot of parents will wring their hands over exposing their little angels to this very ugly side of life. But the bottom line is, do you really care about your kids or not? You cannot consider any child immune to the seductive call of getting high, especially if they are having problems fitting in with day to day school life. If they are going to lose their lives to addiction, at least let them do so with their eyes wide open. This kind of reality based and reliable information will raise a red flag in their heads when they hear the words; "Just try this. It won't hurt much and it's a lot of fun. It's what really cool people are doing. You want to be cool, don't you?"

Hard drugs, however, are just one more piece in the mosaic of social chaos. Anyone who has spent years working in the emergency medical setting can catalogue an almost endless supply of irresponsible, selfish, pathetic, bizarre and criminal human activity. However, once the shocking impact of those stories wears off, the question remains what can be done to reduce the incidence of that bad behavior? Answering this question is a very tall order. Attempting to address the problem of human shortcomings on a massive scale requires having enough insight to be able to go wherever the unpleasant truths about these problems might lead. This isn't as easy as one might think. Towards that end, I am going to suggest six basic attitudes and insights that should help clarify one's thinking when approaching the mammoth and complex problems created by chaotic living. To begin with, perhaps the most important attitude necessary when approaching society's dysfunctionality is one of true humility. Degrading others accomplishes nothing. Moralistic clichés designed to make ourselves feel superior have no place in approaching problems of this magnitude. Often my own snap judgments of E.R. patients turned out to be completely wrong once I got to know those patients better. Usually I could find a common thread of humanity that I could use as a bridge between them and myself. As professional health providers, we learned over time that the best medicine is delivered if it is done in a non judgmental fashion. In that sense the emergency room is not the place to try to change the direction of society. But what used to drive our medical team crazy was how destructive patterns of behavior were repeated again and again with no end in sight. Being exposed to that on a daily basis was truly discouraging.

In addition to humility, the second attitude that is essential in addressing social disaster is the determination to be brutally honest. You cannot be afraid to discuss anything. No ideology, theology or cherished views can be considered off limits to a clear and penetrating evaluation.

At this point I have to give credit to my former closest friend for being an example of applying clear and honest thinking to problem solving. His name was Doug and he lived a truly remarkable life. When Doug was just two years old his dad abandoned the family. His mother slid deeply into alcoholism. By the time Doug was eleven years old, he was running the family. He graduated from high school without a dime, but he was a very pragmatic self starter. He joined the military in order to receive advanced training in electronics. That training almost cost him his life when a mortar round in Vietnam blew him through a door.

After the war he made the transition from electronics to computers at a time when major businesses were starting to incorporate information technology. He used his keen observational powers to become an expert trouble shooter for major computer systems, including evaluating a corporate structure's inability to interface itself with a given computer program. He began lecturing nationally on this and related subjects. He built a good marriage. Then one stormy afternoon his jeep flipped and killed him.

Doug spent his relatively short life challenging presumptions. He took nothing for granted when it came to problem solving. His great strength was his ability to creatively observe without prejudice. He would then walk a problem through from beginning to end with relentless logic.

Doug once said to me "Sam, the most important aspect of problem solving is not finding solutions to the problem. The most important aspect of problem solving is being able to clearly define the problem in the first place. Once you have the problem firmly in hand, solutions usually are not that hard to find." Therefore the focus on these huge issues should concentrate on understanding clearly what the problems really are and how we got there in the first place. As previously stated, there is not room for clichés. Every phrase and concept has to be carefully thought through.

As one works through this complex world of social problems essential attitude number three comes into play. We simply cannot allow ourselves to be overwhelmed by the enormity of the problems. One can easily view the chaos in society and simply give up. We used to look at each other in the emergency room after dealing with the latest social catastrophe and say "What can you do?" The problems are so immense that even approaching the issues can seem like attempting to stop the tide from coming in. Every day in emergency room we put our fingers in the leaks in the dyke, but no one was every fixing the dyke. The alternative to addressing these major issues is to continue to let society slowly slide downhill, and that is unacceptable.

The fourth useful insight is that social chaos will never be completely eliminated. The roots of our problems are simply too deep. Generations of people have spent their lives in destructive and selfish life styles. All that can be done with most of these folk is to present them with some positive alternatives to their self destruction. Doing this will pull a few people back from the edge of the abyss, but certainly not everyone.

In addition to presenting positive alternatives to chaotic lifestyles, one should never reward those whose actions have a destructive effect on society. Every time a law or social policy is enacted that will influence human behavior, the question has to be asked "Will this policy help people to move forward with their lives, or will it enable them to stay in their self-destructive or passive routine?" There are a lot of hound dogs out there just sitting on a nail and howling. Patting them on the head won't accomplish anything.

The last essential awareness is to deeply understand that we are all more or less crazy. We are in many ways a maladaptive species. We keep acting in ways that do not produce a constructive or positive outcome to our problems. Simply put, we keep reliving our mistakes. Many of us lack a creative dynamic that will change our lives for the better.

Earlier I mentioned the first great life lesson I learned which was the analogy of a hound dog sitting on a nail. My second great life lesson arrived courtesy of the U.S. military. About a month into our basic training, two hundred of us found ourselves watching one of the army's many training films. We sat in the dark classroom just glad to be out of the rain and mud for a few minutes. The training film made one simple point. Did you ever notice that the few valuable life guiding principles that you stumble across are usually, in terms of content, not complex at all?

In the film, a handful of actors were dressed as soldiers pretending that they were on the front lines during combat. The enemy shelling had momentarily stopped. Two separate groups of soldiers sitting in their respective fox holes found themselves with some spare time. One group of guys smoked cigarettes and layed around talking about their girlfriends and baseball. The second group of soldiers in the neighboring fox hole never stopped moving. Two guys were filling sand bags which they used to construct a protective wall around the top of their fox hole. The rest of the team dug the fox hole much deeper. They also took some spare planks of wood and made a crude floor in the fox hole to keep their feet dry. Then they took an eight inch wide clay section of pipe and inserted it into the lowest point of the fox hole floor. The pipe was angled down and away from the center of the fox hole. The idea was that if some unfriendly individual lobbed a grenade into your fox hole, you would kick it into the pipe. Since the body of the pipe was buried in the ground next to the fox hole, the resulting explosion would hurt no one as long as you kept away from the opening of the pipe. This was a basic lesson drawn from years of trench warfare.

The film continued and of course the mortar shells started falling again. The guys in the shallow unimproved fox hole were completely unprepared, although in real life it is amazing how many guys you can get into a shallow fox hole when the mortar shells come raining down. But the soldiers in the much improved fox hole were better prepared and safer.

As the camera showed the obvious difference between the two situations, the film's narrator said "Men, when in combat never just sit around. Instead, always use your spare time to improve your position."

The images in that film never left me. No, I do not have the ultimate fox hole in my English rose garden, although when family issues become really strained, it doesn't seem like such a bad idea. Instead, when I wake up in the morning I ask myself one simple question, "What can I do today to improve my position in life?" If I am able to identify even a small task that will move me in a forward direction, that task becomes the goal for the day. This is not just compulsive behavior. This is a survival tactic.

Up to this point we have examined the horrendous problems that result from chaotic living, while at the same time exploring attitudes and perspectives that may be useful while attempting to evaluate solutions to these problems. Now I am going to postulate three fundamental courses of action without which significant social change is unlikely to occur. These courses of action are costly, painful and difficult. But changing the fundamental fabric of society is never easy.

POSTULATE NO.1

Whatever you do, do not subsidize childbirth. Young single girls who do not have the life experience, financial resources or emotional stability to adequately parent children create the milieu out of which social chaos both continues and multiplies. In short, girls who cannot even take care of themselves have no business being mothers.

Granted, some young single mothers do make good parents. But if a child ends up by being raised by a dedicated single mom, it is the exception rather than the rule. Often the guidelines for life are handed out not by a parent, but instead by local gang leaders. It's also worthwhile to realize that a good single mother is a better bet than a couple of married drunks. Holy matrimony in and of itself does not automatically confer adequate parenting skills.

It obviously seems heartless to just cut off child funding. But I am not trying to take away money from children who are already here. Instead, all that needs to be done is to announce that public funding of child birth will stop in eleven months. That way women who are already pregnant can get in under the wire. Welfare payments to existing children would continue.

It's also useful to realize that payments to unwed mothers were originally initiated by good hearted people who wanted to cover the occasional accidental pregnancy. But over the decades unwed motherhood has become a viable career option. That, combined with the explosion of the illicit drug market, really puts society on the skids. I am not talking here about lifestyles that I find personally distasteful. I am talking about lifestyles that result in an unrelenting series of tragedies. A trial judge in England recently bemoaned the loss of adequate parenting within society. He said "Not everyone from a broken home becomes a criminal, but all the criminals I see are from broken homes."

Unfortunately, stopping welfare payments to mothers will result in more people living under bridges. That aspect of changing social policy seems cruel, but in the long term human suffering will be reduced. Then, and only then, could a really remarkable possibility occur. Maybe, just maybe, people will have babies because they actually want them and can adequately care for them. That's a concept so staggering to me that envisioning it within my mind is very difficult. I mean, even birds build a nest prior to laying their eggs. But a significant number of our population seems incapable of even the most rudimentary planning and preparation for having a child. Instead, more than fifty percent of the time, "If it happens, it happens."

I'm not suggesting completely turning our backs on the down and outs. We need to keep on with food stamps, soup kitchens, food banks, shelters, charitable organizations, social services and free clinics. Remember, no one starves to death, no one freezes to death.

But we need to move way beyond just cutting welfare funding. Society's entire attitude towards childbirth has to change. As it now stands if a man sperm donors five or six kids by different women, he just forgets it all happened and moves on. No one says a word. A clear and direct message has to be spread throughout the local communities that sperm donoring and then abandoning a baby is a cruel and cowardly thing to do, which is the simple truth.

In order to communicate a community wide message about responsible parenting effectively, peer pressure has to be brought into play. Make no mistake about it; peer pressure is a very valuable tool when it comes to influencing human behavior. For example, a young man will go to war for no other reason than the fact all the other young men in his neighborhood are going to that same war. It's all part of the herd instinct and the need to belong to the tribe. But harnessing this need to belong so that it moves society away from destructive life styles requires a genuine debate on our common ethical issues so that applied peer pressure can speak clearly and with one voice. As stated in the section on religion, it's important that the edicts handed out through peer pressure are not formulated by some charismatic psychopath. But that's the basic strength of any democracy; we can actually hold an open forum on the issues that affect all of us. The important thing is to initiate and continue the debate on these moral issues.

From a practical viewpoint as seen from standing in the center of an emergency room, our social value system is approaching extinction. Instead of dealing with the problem of vanishing ethics, our communities seem to place all their efforts into avoiding offending anyone. It's high time for us to use peer pressure in ways that will help connect people to the consequences of their actions.

POSTULATE NO. 2

Take back the schools. Metal detectors, security forces, strict discipline, whatever it takes. No more messing about. The students have to clearly understand that without a good education that leads to a marketable skill, life will be difficult, frustrating and often short.

If a kid repeatedly acts out in class, a clear message should be given by the other students to that individual that he or she is interrupting their collective chance for a better life. There will always be a class clown (I was one) or a rebel, and that's not all bad. But the kids don't seem to understand that education is an opportunity, not a game. If you want security, stability and prosperity in your life, you have to work for it. There is no easy way out of this reality, unless you invent the hula hoop.

We've already discussed the plight of the working poor family. Let's enlarge that discussion with the following illustration. Please understand that anyone who brings home a pay check has my respect. I've seen border line retarded people or those with serious post traumatic brain injury still managing to show up every day on time for work. Reliable people like these often hold entire families together. But if you move boxes from the factory floor onto pallets which the fork lift then loads onto a truck, then you are in a very vulnerable position. One serious illness, prolonged back injury or a company lay off and you're unemployed. But if you know how to fix the engines on those forklifts, and the entire production line slows down if you're not there to fix those engines, then you are in a much more secure position. In addition to better job security, you're also making about three times as much money as the box movers. Bills have to be paid and you want to be the person who can pay them.

Without a solid foundation and the three Rs (and a winning smile), it's unlikely that you will ever find yourself in a secure position. Life will then become a series of low paying, often short term jobs. Boredom then sets in, and drugs and alcohol begin to have a strong appeal. You find yourself living for the weekend game of pool in the bar with your friends. You also know that there is never adequate money to properly cloth, shelter and feed your wife and kids. You find yourself looking for some exciting extra marital affairs just to put some meaning (or danger) into your life.

Students in school think the good times will never end. They don't see life's coming trials and insecurities. Instead, they are just doing the day. There is simply no sense of urgency. What needs to happen is an injection of insight into why most of what they are learning actually matters. In other words, they have to see the big picture. Once the students have that insight, then they can pressure other students into developing a team spirit that has everyone working together for common goals.

Understanding the long term value of a useful education helps kids bridge the gap between being a child and becoming an adult. But it's not enough for this motivational message to be put forth by adults alone. If the kids only hear about the need to focus on education from adults, they will think the uncool, uptight old farts are just mouthing off again. The students have to understand from square one that the purpose of a good education is to build a happy and fulfilling life. Granted, everybody has to define "happy and fulfilling" for themselves. But although there is no iron clad approach to that happiness, we can give the students valuable insights from our own experiences. They really need those hard earned lessons learned from adult experiences and mistakes. These triumphs and mistakes can add depth to kid's understanding of the behaviors that tend to enrich life, as opposed to those behaviors that often have damaging results. Being able to separate what works in life from what doesn't work is a crucial part of growing up.

In order for peer pressure to function effectively, entire families have to focus on the kid's education. Given the dysfuntionality of most families, that kind of team work presents a real challenge. But strict standards of behavior have to be set. The kids must know they are to be home at a certain hour at night, and the homework must be done before they go to bed. Again this sounds like boring and predictable advice, but I've seen the painful results of bad behavior and it's not pretty.

Some students become very discouraged early on because they are simply not good at academics. These kids have to understand that future employers don't all want Albert Einsteins. What employers want are employees who are reliable and can work with others. Communities need to construct vehicles of education that will help students make the most of what they have, as well as allowing them to feel good about their accomplishments. Some school systems may pay so much attention to the high achiever that they leave the average or below average student behind.

Interestingly enough, there is another side to this story. I've lived in an affluent suburb where the high powered, anal, caffeine driven soccer moms placed unrelenting pressure on their kids to be number one in everything. Kids in their early years don't know how to handle that kind of pressure. You can see them milling about in a sea of anxiety that will lead them eventually to Valium, vodka martini lunches, eating disorders, or just a good old fashioned series of panic attacks. Throughout all this motivational stuff, it is crucially important to allow a kid to just be a kid.

The peer pressure most needed now is in the inner city schools. The whole concept of what it is to be "cool" needs to be redefined. Again team work and moving towards clearly defined goals are the key to making anything work.

And what about the quality of teaching those inner city kids receive? Here's a good idea. First, clearly define which schools are truly underserved, both inner city and rural. Then find energetic and committed teachers who have a good track record in education and offer them combat pay in addition to their regular salary if they will work in an underserved area. But getting good teachers alone is not enough. Local communities have to back those teachers up. Teachers can't teach if the classroom is in chaos. As stated before, strict standards of behavior have to be set and enforced. I've talked to teachers who actually feared for their own safety within schools. Why have we let things degenerate to that level?

So where's all the money going to come from to fund all of these changes? After all, every school system is into the penny jar at the end of the budget year. Well, it's all very simple. We have spent multiple billions of dollars over the last decade on the war on terror. No one with a brain would argue that terrorism does not present a clear and present danger.

But the descent of our culture into self destructive and irresponsible chaos represents a far greater threat to our society than terrorism. If the money can be found for the war on terror (and now to bail out greedy bankers) adequate money can be found to revitalize our educational system.

It's also a shame that there aren't any massive oil reserves located under the inner cities. If those oil reserves existed, a lot of money would move to underserved areas very quickly.

POSTULATE NO. 3

Zero Tolerance is a must. Any government that cannot make the streets reasonably safe has failed in its primary mission. As soon as anyone says this however, some people jump up and down yelling about a police state and Big Brother taking over. To them, the S.S. troops are always just behind the bushes. But why should citizens walk the streets in fear? Why are our elderly placed in serious jeopardy from street violence? Why do school buses get hit by stray bullets? Why does an individual who stands up to gang violence get kicked to death? Why is a kid afraid to smile in his own neighborhood? The list of atrocities goes on and on. These horrible things happen because we allow them to happen. Our society funds life styles that give rise to criminal behavior, and then wont fund an adequate police service to deal with the resulting carnage. Entire neighborhoods are under the control of gangs. Why doesn't the war on terror contain an assault on organized crime and street gangs? We could wait a long time to be hit by weapons of mass destruction (hopefully), but street violence is with us right now. We just wall ourselves off from that part of life, until it hits us. And that's the essence of the problem. Until we clearly understand that we and our loved ones are all potential victims of street violence, we won't be adequately motivated to enforce zero tolerance.

In previous pages I have described what it was like to live in New York City in the 1970s. You just kept your head down and hoped you didn't get mugged. I couldn't wait to get out of there. It was like being a wildebeest in a large herd. There was safety in numbers, but you could see predators and scavengers on all sides.

About ten years after zero tolerance was instituted, a friend of mine twisted my arm into paying a return visit to New York City. I couldn't believe the difference. No large city is completely devoid of danger, but the whole attitude on the streets had changed. The pervasive mood of fear was gone. Outside of the occasional and intensely muttering psychotic (or was it someone with a cell phone bolted to the side of their head?) the biggest danger was finding yourself standing between a hyper manic executive and the local coffee shop.

Elderly former New Yorkers are moving back to the city of their birth because they have a good chance of not suffering a broken hip from being thrown to the ground by a mugger. I just walked around the streets of New York City in simple astonishment. For the first time I saw what a dramatic change can be brought about in a community just by force of will. New York City decided to change for the better and it did. In addition to effective law enforcement, I think the tragic events of 9/11 galvanized New Yorkers into a stronger sense of who they are.

From my current home I can look across the rolling green farmer's fields of the English countryside. The biggest danger here is facing a huge tractor coming the other way on a one lane country road. Life between the thick hedgerows that line both sides of these rural roads can get very interesting. But England is a culture in rapid change. The country is flooded with immigrants looking for:

No.1: A better life through hard work.
No.2: Political asylum
No.3: A free ride
No.4: A way to expand their organized criminal empire
No.5: A nice internet tea room where they can plan their next Jihad.

Britain is indeed an interesting and culturally rich mix.

Through all of its recent cultural change the British government has taken an interesting approach to criminal violence. The powers that be have decided that using "excessive force" to stop a crime is in itself a crime. For instance, if you stop someone from stealing your car and in the process hit him, you can be sued or go to jail for using "excessive force". British culture has decided that the physical well being of a criminal is more important than whatever he steals. Now that's a novel approach to law enforcement. It represents an effort to keep everything nice, tidy and sanitized. Unfortunately real life rarely works that way.

But in all fairness, you wouldn't want to inflict irreversible brain damage on a kid who was stealing your bicycle. It is possible to apply common sense to some situations.

There is also less gun violence in England than in their armed-to-the-teeth former western colony. But the incidence of violent crime in England is rapidly on the rise. I am beginning to see things here that I used to see in New York City. Knife crime is out of control and street gangs do rule some areas. The resulting increase of both "wrong places" and "wrong times" into which a British citizen can unexpectedly walk has made everyone feel more vulnerable. The rule of law here is indeed tenuous and the criminals know that.

All of this presents British society with a real problem. The average citizen is reluctant to stop a crime in progress because he might get stabbed or he might go to jail for using excessive force. One criminal case that highlighted this issue involved an older man who lived in a relatively remote home in the English countryside. He endured one break in and robbery after another. The local police were too spread out in this rural area to adequately monitor his home. He put in traps, alarms and lookout posts to try to protect his property. He lived in fear, sleeping in his clothes with a loaded shotgun at his side. He had lost thousands of pounds during the previous multiple burglaries.

As expected, he once again awoke to the sounds of a break in. He went downstairs and shot both burglars. One burglar, a teenager with several criminal convictions, was fatally wounded. His companion, who was older and had 30 prior criminal convictions, was seriously wounded in the leg. Both burglars managed to flee, but the young man's body was found in a field the next day.

At this point, people who live in the United States should sit down before they read the next sentence. The British courts ruled that the farmer had used excessive force in preventing the burglary. They convicted the farmer of murder and gave him a mandatory life sentence. The presiding judge said "The law is that every citizen is entitled to use reasonable force to prevent crime. Burglary is a crime and a householder in his own home may think he is being reasonable. But he may not be reasonable and that can have tragic consequences".

Got that?

The surviving burglar is currently suing the farmer for injuries suffered as a result of using excessive force, The B.B.C. paid the burglar £4,000 for an interview.

On appeal, the farmer got a reduced sentence. But the parole board refused to grant him early release. Because he showed no remorse for his crime, the parole board felt that the farmer *continued to be a threat to future burglars!* The farmer now sleeps in his car.

But not to worry. After months of thinking about this dilemma, I've come up with a solution to the problem of using excessive force against criminals. This solution takes a bit of planning, but with determination and a good public relations campaign, it can become a solid reality.

Almost every standard house in England has a closet under the stairs (just ask Harry Potter). On the inside of the door to this closet, the home owner should place a board containing eight hooks. Each hook would hold a different appropriate force device (hereafter known as an "A.F.D."). The eight hooks would represent eight different grades of malevolent intent on the part of the intruder. For example, a level 1 malevolent intent (M.I. No.1.) would consist of idle curiosity about what architectural features exist within the house. An appropriate A.F.D. for an M.I.No.1 break in would be a feather duster (to tickle the intruder). The grades of malevolent intent would increase in severity until you reach an M.I.No.8. A typical motivation behind an M.I.No.8 break in would be to rape and murder every member of the family and then eat the bodies in a fit of orgiastic glee over the next three days. An appropriate M.I.No.8 A.F.D. would be a neighborhood approved, environmentally friendly, low carbon footprint and smokeless mini-bazooka. But wait a minute. I distinctly remember a clause in the British excessive force statute that prohibits bazookas. Therefore, the M.I. No.8 A.F.D. would have to be a single barrel semi-automatic shotgun fitted with a barrel clip and an infra-red Starlight night vision scope with laser sights. That should do the trick. Converting a simple shotgun into the equivalent of an anti-aircraft battery would also greatly increase the take home count at the next pheasant shoot. But it would really stress out the retriever dogs. They wouldn't know which way to turn next. A few dogs might actually be lost to falling birds.

But having eight available A.F.D.'s alone is not enough. The criminal malevolent intent must be appropriately and accurately assessed in order for the system to function smoothly. Toward that end, a large manual needs to be kept on a shelf next to the A.F.D.'s. This manual would allow any given intruder to correctly indicate his M.I. level in advance of any A.F.D. choice by the home owner. That necessitates the homeowner sitting down with the manual and the criminal and explaining at length the eight levels of M.I. It's important at this point not to startle or agitate the intruder. This is a crucial time for clear thinking and factual analysis. This manual would have to be multi-lingual allowing for the intruder's possible foreign birth. It would also have to be full of relevant pictures and diagrams in case either the intruder or the home owner is illiterate. Initially there may be some confusion, but with purposeful determination and mutual co-operation a successful conclusion almost always can be reached. At some point the intruder can, with definitive conviction, take his right index finger and point to the appropriate M.I. diagram. The home owner should ask "Final answer?" Then the home owner can ask the intruder to hold the manual while the home owner goes to the closet and chooses the appropriate A.F.D. Hopefully all of this can be concluded before the intruder kills the home owner. But even this doesn't have to be a serious problem. If during negotiations with the intruder it appears that the M.I. level is going to be a six or greater (which means that someone is going to die), the index to the manual could contain a rapid decision making algorithm which would streamline the pathway to a successful M.I. determination. But the rapid decision making algorithm should only be used in appropriate situations. Unnecessary haste in these emotionally charged confrontations could lead to unfortunate and costly errors in judgment.

Killing another human being is a horrendous and irreversible thing to do. But leaving people unsure of how to defend themselves in the face of criminal activity represents a massive failure on the part of government. Some people might argue that in a civilized society people should not get shot. But felons are not civilized people. They will hurt you in order to get what they want. You and your loved ones are just in their way. Remember, the motivation for a significant number of burglaries is to get money for drugs. If the burglar is in acute drug withdrawal, whatever inhibitory impulses they have against violence will be muted. Then there are the sadists. I don't think we have to go into great detail on that.

Here's a simple concept. If you don't want to get shot, don't break into someone's house in the middle of the night. That concept puts the responsibility for harm back on the criminal's shoulders. That's the way it should be. The above mentioned farmer underwent what amounts to terrorism, and it still goes on. We are all potential targets.

If I ever saw a country that needs zero tolerance, it's England. Don't get me wrong. If you commit murder or multiple rapes in England, Scotland Yard will relentlessly track you down. But it takes a major crime to extend the long arm of the law. The routine car thefts, break ins and muggings get recorded but not much happens. For one thing, police officers are bogged down with hours and hours of paperwork every time they make an arrest. That alone will reduce an officer's motivation to make that arrest. Also, every hour that a cop is sitting in front of a word processor is an hour he is not out patrolling the streets.

I'm not a criminologist, so I am going to make this very short. What zero tolerance has taught us is that if you accept crime that is relatively low in severity, the volume of serious crime overall will increase. Emergency rooms will fill up with victims. Criminal activity on all levels has to be stopped as well as social policies that give rise to criminal behavior. It takes a tremendous amount of political will to turn these simple ideas into action. The realization that in terms of the end results, violent crime and terrorism are indistinguishable from each other should act to focus those efforts.

At this point if you are American go pour yourself a Kentucky Bourbon over ice. If you are English pour yourself a Pimms, or if you are an alcoholic anonymous charter member, pour yourself a diet Coke with ice and a slice of lemon. These two chapters have dragged you through some of the uglier sides of life, although believe me, what we've discussed is just the tip of the socially dysfunctional iceberg. Now it's time to take a deep breath and regroup.

When all is said and done, can we actually fix any of the previously discussed social problems? In my more cynical moments, I think not. After all, our collective bad behavior is rooted in who we are as a species, and what can you do about that? For most of us just getting through the day is tough enough, much less tackling these immense social difficulties. But these problems just won't go away. A lot of people have to live every day of their lives with the consequences of our social dysfunctionality.

The bottom line to me is that we are all still somewhat in charge of our collective destiny. There are challenges we simply have to face. The equivalent of Adolf Hitler will rise again, plagues will recur and our common social failures will always be in our face. Like it or not, we will ultimately be defined by how we meet these challenges. We must grab the rudder and pray for enough honest insight to guide our course. The alternative to correcting our social bad behavior is to careen randomly through the rapids, and that's what gets me the most. The forces of chaos are dictating what happens to us and no one seems to care. So, although the previously mentioned three postulates may seem boring, predictable and I am sure fascist to some, at least it's a beginning.

The primary goal of this book is to start a dialogue about the problems and values that affect us all. If nothing more happens than we get off our collective butts and begin to make a positive difference in our local communities, then I'm satisfied.

Finally, please understand that I did not come to these postulates and insights by reading some right wing pamphlet. Instead, I simply observed the results of chaotic living every day I worked in the emergency room. Every damned day.

Chapter XV

PARTING SHOTS

This chapter contains a patchwork quilt of thoughts and observations that didn't easily fit under other topics. Approach this as you would a selection of appetizers on a menu. Take a bite of each and come to your own conclusions.

ON HOMOSEXUALITY

The issues of gay rights, gay marriage, etc. are currently all over the newspapers. The Episcopal Church has been shaken to its foundations by the ordination of an openly gay bishop. The religious right actively campaigns against this "sin." According to them homosexuality can be purged from the human personality by sincere confession, spiritual cleansing and religious education.

Turning to the Bible, Jesus had little or nothing to say about homosexuality. Paul the Apostle, one of the most creative and articulate theological minds in history, condemns homosexuality in three of his letters (Romans 1:26-27, 1st Corinthians 6: 9-10 and 1st Timothy 1: 9-10). If I am understanding Paul correctly, he sees homosexuality as running against the natural order of things, which was ordained by God.

Paul the Apostle was wrong. Homosexuality reliably appears in roughly four to ten percent of the male population in almost all societies and across all cultures, except where they are killed, like in Iran. When President Armadinajad spoke at Columbia University, he was asked about the treatment of gays in Iran. His response was "There are no homosexuals in Iran." How can anyone be that deliberately deluded? It scares me that the President of a major country can be that out to lunch.

Let's get real. Having worked in religion and medicine for thirty years I was constantly exposed to the gay community. My seminary had a separate gay floor and lesbian floor. Gay nurses are everywhere. These individuals all had one thing in common; they all helped other people. My experience is that bad people do not make a profession out of helping others.

In talking with psychotherapists, I learned that there are two basic types of homosexuality:

No.1: The patient had a series of horrible experiences with the mothering figure and cannot be close to women. This is not true homosexuality and needs intensive psychotherapy.

No.2: There are those who are born homosexuals. The religious right is donning sack cloth and ashes as I speak, but homosexuality is part of God's plan. I mean ten percent of the male population turning out this way cannot be an accident.

True homosexuals know at a very early age that they are different. The opposite sex just doesn't do it for them. They may go through a period of intense denial about who they are. In fact most of the ultra conservative religious leaders who aggressively persecute gays are themselves closet homosexuals. Otherwise it is difficult to explain their intense rage.

The media, rating prostitutes that they are, often don't help the situation. Wouldn't a televised reasoned debate between members of the religious right and the gay community be interesting and informative? Will you see that on prime time television? No way, José. But when the gay pride parade prances its way through the streets of San Francisco, the prime time cameras are focused and ready to go. They immediately zoom in on the most flaming and flaky characters they can find. Somewhere in Iowa there is a man in his mid forties sitting on a couch watching the evening news. His old tee shirt barely covers his pot belly. He has a cigar in his mouth and a beer in his right hand. When the images of a gay pride parade flash across his TV screen his jaw drops and his cigar falls into his lap. He yells to his wife, "Ella May, drop what you are doing, come here and take a look at *this!*" Like I said, it's all about the ratings.

There are sexual predators within the gay community. There are sexual predators in all walks of life and society must constantly be vigilant for their activity. But most gays just want to get through the day and get on with life. In that way they are just like the rest of us.

But the lives of gay people are not easy. Gay individuals bond together into groups for mutual support and protection. They are often attacked by those outside of their community. Families frequently are torn apart when a son or daughter turns out to be gay or lesbian. Some families can accept their children for who they are, others cannot.

Putting all the debate about the roots of homosexuality to one side, our behavior towards the gay community is what really matters. What does the heterosexual segment of our society gain by violently ostracizing homosexuals? Like it or not, homosexuals make major contributions to every aspect of our society and culture. They certainly aren't going away. Allowing homosexuals to live in peace doesn't mean that heterosexuals need to like or adopt the gay lifestyle. It's only for a few. But whatever our views towards homosexuality, what matters most is that we just leave them alone.

SPIN

During the past few decades we have openly recognized a segment of society that always existed, but stayed somewhat in the shadows. I am referring of course to the "spin doctors." Now there's an interesting group of folk.

So, what is spin? As near as I can figure, spin involves manipulating and distorting the truth so that the resulting words will have a premeditated and desired effect on public opinion. Or, to rephrase that same concept, spin doctors are professional liars.

What does a spin doctor say to his kids when they ask "Daddy what do you do for a living?" I wish the responses to that question could be secretly recorded. Do you think the kids ever get a straight answer?

When I first heard about spin doctors I found myself wondering how we could have allowed standards of behavior to sink so low. But then I realized there was no reason to be completely negative about "spin." For one thing, it's now all out in the open. Everyone knows that spin doctors exist and what they do. In fact such total candor about the subject could open up a whole new lucrative career pathway. English departments and institutions of higher learning could go way beyond "Greatest British Authors", and offer a course entitled "SPIN – 101". Furthermore, it certainly wouldn't be much of a stretch for law schools to openly teach spin. After all, the average lawyer's song and dance in court certainly contains an element of spin. In fact, the more I think about this, the more I see unlimited potential.

Imagine if you will a family reunion. Uncle Ted is talking to his nephew Tommy. The conversation might go as follows:

Ted: Great to see you Tommy; it's been years since we last spoke. What have you been doing with yourself?

Tommy: I'm at University.

Ted: What are you studying?

Tommy: I'm doing a doctorate in level 3 spin.

Ted: That's sounds challenging. What does "level 3 spin" mean?

Tommy: It means I'm trained to lie to my boss as well as the general public.

Ted: Why would you lie to the man who is signing your pay check?

Tommy: The purpose of lying to one's boss is to maintain the boss's inflated sense of self importance.

Ted: What difference does that make?

Tommy: If a boss loses his sense of inflated self importance, then he won't feel so motivated to lie to the public, and I'll be out of a job.

Ted: That makes sense.

Tommy: Yeh, I wanted to do level 4 spin, but I didn't think I could lie convincingly in three different languages.

Ted: That does sound tough.

Tommy: You bet. Level 4 spinners have to be able to twist historical events in multiple major cultures. Even humor is important. What's funny in Kenya is not funny in Japan. Level 4 students are up all night trying to sort this stuff out. You have to clearly understand what's actually going on in a culture before you can distort that reality to your advantage.

Ted: Are there even higher levels of spin?

Tommy: Actually, level 5 spin does exist, but no one talks about it.

Ted: How are your grades?

Tommy: Well, that's been a source of mild frustration.

Ted: What do you mean?

Tommy: When I ask about my grades I can't get a straight answer from my professors.

Ted: So you have no idea how you are doing?

Tommy: Actually I have had some good feedback. One professor told me that I'm doing a whole lot better than many people who have much less ability than I do. I mean, I just have to see that in a positive light. Another professor told me that all my grades are within just a few points off two standard deviations from the mean. That has to be above average, right?

Ted: Do these courses of study lay down any ethical guidelines for you?

Tommy: Of course they do! Every morning prior to starting our class work, we repeat our motto: "Reality is relative, and the truth is a tool."

Ted: This all sounds good. What do you think the future holds?

Tommy: The sky is the limit. Spin doctors are now talking about forming a union like the Screen Writer's Guild. Can you envision how strong an organization like that could be? Imagine how powerful a strike threat would be just prior to a Presidential election?

Ted: This is all very exciting.

Tommy: Uncle Ted how's your career as a Tobacco lobbyist going?

Ted: To be honest things have tailed off a bit since the big law suits. I'm thinking about a lateral career change. In fact, tell me more about level 4 spin. Did you know I'm fluent in several Chinese and Indian dialects? That's where the tobacco companies are currently pushing their products.

Tommy: So things are slow on the home front?

Ted: Well, there are bright spots. With the resurgence of the Cold War the tobacco companies are really doing their bit for Uncle Sam.

Tommy: How so?

Ted: If the Russians keep smoking at current levels, almost no one will live long enough to make the rank of General in the Russian Army.

Tommy: Uncle Ted, you really know how to put things into perspective. I think you have a solid future in spin. Refill your champagne glass and sit over here. I'm going to fill you in on a whole new world.

Advice to young girls; "Before you marry a man, sleep with him and see him drunk once."

On a family member expressing dismay upon realizing that no one missed a recently departed elderly relative, "Grief, like love, has to be earned."

"Some people just cannot be happy. Other people will find ways to be happy even in adverse circumstances. But a significant percentage of the population, regardless of their life situation, will always find something to worry about".

"It is a sad truth that in this world, you cannot negotiate from a position of weakness."

"They are all the same people! Terrorists, Nazis, religious extremists, Arian supremacists, they are all the same people!" I said "You have to explain that." She said, "If you plot the general population on a two standard deviations type graph, you'll find on the extreme left the tree huggers and the "give peace a chance" people. Towards the centre of the bell curve you will find most of the rest of the population. Then on the extreme right you have a group of people who are very inflexible in their thinking. For them, everything has to be presented in black and white. When you disturb their concrete interpretation of life, they tend to respond with violent outbursts of emotion. They know that society will not understand or condone their violent behavior on an individual basis, so they tend to join movements that justify their need for violence. All of the extremist groups are full of these people. They also have one additional mode of thinking in common. I said "What's that?" She replied "Whenever something bad happens in these people's lives, they are always convinced that it is someone else's fault."

"Consciousness comes out of complexity." This statement arose out of a conversation with our teenage daughter about biochemical reactions in the human body. "If you create a system complex enough to integrate and evaluate an almost infinite number of possibilities, then consciousness evolves. The whole literally becomes more than the sum of its parts. An earth worm for example does not contemplate its day, but rather responds to its preprogrammed biological routine. But a human being is so complex that it gives rise to consciousness. This leads me to believe that the creator of the universe is a mathematician".

After a sumptuous Lebanese dinner in London, "There's no adequate reason why all of the countries in the world couldn't get along. Then we could all exchange recipes."

"If you have to twist yourself mentally into a pretzel to make your theology 'work', then your theology probably isn't true."

A FINAL WORD ON RELIGION

These are difficult and confusing times for religious people. Crazy ideology and crazy people abound, each trying to gather more followers for the cause. It seems almost impossible to distil out human lunacy from mass religious movements. Many religious people choose to go it alone, and I really can't blame them. Its far better to be alone in your faith knowing that you haven't compromised your convictions, than to be swept away by religious fervor that is nothing more than a mask for the religious leader's neurosis. No matter what path you take, thinking for yourself is always the most difficult, but ultimately the most rewarding way to go.

I shared these feelings and concerns with an old friend of mine from seminary who is still active in the ministry. She said "You know, I think some of the American Indian religions came closest to the truth." I responded "Please elaborate." She continued, "The American Indian believes that every human being has a spirit guide. The religious person's life's work is to connect to that spirit guide." This is indeed a creative approach to faith. The huge upside of this kind of individually tailored religious freedom is that religiously sanctioned murder would be an unlikely event. In other words the body count should level off.

But how does one then infuse everyday life with religious energy, while at the same time avoiding the previously mentioned human failings? Not too long ago I had a conversation with one of the nurses who still works at my home hospital. She related the story of an elderly couple; we will call them George and Marie. George developed a serious bone infection. Bone infections are very difficult to treat because the blood supply to bones is limited. Without a good blood supply it's very hard to get antibiotics to the infection's source. In this case, surgical debridement wasn't going to help much. Therefore, George had to come to our emergency room for I.V. antibiotic therapy twice a day for six weeks. But there were problems. George lived a significant distance from the hospital and was no longer able to drive. Thus George had to lean on the good intentions of his neighbors to get him to and from the hospital. The two treatments and travel could take up as much as four hours each day. There was also a glitch in George's health insurance that would only pay for any antibiotic treatments if they were done in the hospital. Even a bigger problem was that Marie was terminally ill with cancer. She and George were very close. They loved to spend their retirement years together travelling through the United States. George was now Marie's primary care giver and he was terrified that his wife would die alone while he was at the hospital getting his treatments.

But with the help of George's neighbors, the antibiotic therapy was completed and, at least initially, things looked good. Then a month later he developed a fever and bone pain. The infection had recurred. The orthopedic specialist concluded that another six weeks of I.V. antibiotic therapy was the best course of treatment. But by now Marie was really sick and could die any day.

Finally the nurses put their collective heads together and said "Enough of this!" They pooled what little money they had and purchased some I.V. antibiotics. Then they called the hospital's risk manager. They asked "If we go out and give the antibiotic I.V. therapy to George in his home, will we lose our jobs?" The risk manager said "Oh, you can't do *that*!!! Your malpractice insurance won't cover you outside the hospital! So, when you do go out and give the antibiotics, for God's sake *don't* screw it up!"

So, on their own time, the nurses delivered the antibiotic therapy to George at his home. During the next six weeks, Marie finally died. When she did pass away, her beloved husband was at her side.

If you want to be close to God, don't bother studying rituals or doctrines. You can argue the rights and wrongs of that stuff ad infinitum and get lost in the details. If you want to be close to God, just do the right thing for no other reason than it is the right thing to do. If human suffering is reduced even slightly as a result of your actions, then you are probably in the right place. It is my statement of faith that in these situations, God will be with you. It's important to note that you will not necessarily be protected. Some lunatic could still kill you. The God that allowed Auschwitz to happen will not stop any evil action. But at least you and the people you are helping will not be alone, and from a religious and humanitarian point of view, that's what matters most. You will also grow, and in this context, there is almost no limit to that growth. Always stay open to new ideas; and if you're not a psycho, trust your gut. It will lead you in the right direction.

EPILOGUE

England, October 2008

Well, whadayaknow! I'm four and a half years out from intensive radiation therapy for recurrent cancer and there is no sign of the disease. I did not expect this to be the course of events. When I retired from medical practice, I thought I was terminally ill. The odds were really against me.

When things were looking really grim, I did my best to come to grips with my own impending death. To be completely honest with you, I only had limited success in that endeavor. It was all just a bit too close for comfort.

Health wise I'm by no means completely out of the woods, and as my age advances, there will be other medical surprises waiting for me. But when I wake up in the morning and the sun shines through the window, I allow myself to think that I actually have a future. What a difference that makes. What a gift, full of possibilities.

So, there are a few good pieces of cheese on the counter along with grapes, crackers and a bottle of Cabernet that has just reached maturity. The English rain has *finally* stopped and the air has a washed clean smell to it. A few gold autumn leaves are twirling in the breeze in a far corner of the garden. The dog looks up at me hoping for either a piece of cheddar (his favorite) or a walk. To him it's all about the basics. I will see that he gets both.

You know, I think I'll just kick back for a while and enjoy this wonderful life.

POST EPILOGUE

April 2009, England

I've got a great idea. I'm going to produce and market a brand new breakfast cereal called "Kredit Krunchy". It will be composed of a combination of puffed wheat and puffed rice, mostly air. Each box will contain a small Madoff action figure in an orange jump suit. The box will also contain one share of Citi Corp. stock which can double as a napkin. The really neat thing is that when milk is added, the cereal completely dissolves. As a result, amazed children can sit around the morning breakfast table and exclaim "It's gone! It disappeared! It was supposed to be there! It's magic!"

Maybe I'll even add a rubber dead cat to the box. The kids can watch it bounce.